SUCCESS AS A CSR

LLOYD FINCH

CRISP PUBLICATIONS, INC.
MENLO PARK, CA

SUCCESS AS A CSR

LLOYD FINCH

CREDITS

Managing Editor: Kathleen Barcos
Editor: Carol Henry
Production: Barbara Atmore
Typesetting: ExecuStaff
Cover Design: Barry Littmann

Copyright © 1998 by Crisp Publications.
Printed in the United States of America by Bawden Printing.

Distribution to the U.S. Trade:

National Book Network, Inc.
4720 Boston Way
Lanham, MD 20706
1-800-462-6420

Library of Congress Catalog Card Number 97-65865
Finch, Lloyd
Success as a CSR
ISBN 1-56052-450-2

To Bunkie

for all his support and energy

CONTENTS

I

FOCUS ON CUSTOMER SERVICE

II

DEVELOPING PROFESSIONALISM

III

THE IMPORTANCE OF KNOWING YOUR CUSTOMER

IV

WORKSHOP: DEVELOPING CUSTOMER SATISFACTION SKILLS

V

MEASURING CSR PERFORMANCE

VI

A MESSAGE
TO THE CSR

ABOUT
THE AUTHOR

BIBLIOGRAPHY

I

FOCUS ON CUSTOMER SERVICE

Customer service careers are available covering a working lifetime—from first job to last. The Customer Service Representative (CSR) job title is one of the fastest growing in the world. And in future years CSRs with advanced skills will enjoy increased responsibility, greater salary, more authority, and enhanced job satisfaction.

Nearly every organization employs CSRs, and the demand for highly skilled CSRs who can provide quality service is growing. As the importance of customer service increases, the skilled CSR will be seen as a significant contributor to a company's success and profits. This translates to even more opportunity for CSR advancement—not only in traditional promotions to supervision or management, but also to high-end CSR positions, such as problem-solving positions or assignment to major or key accounts, national markets, and international accounts.

The only limitations to advancement will be the skill level of the individual CSR. The stronger the individual skills, the greater the opportunity.

This book is about the CSR job and the strategic role played by CSRs in providing quality customer service. We will study ways to be a more successful CSR, and learn a "how-to" approach regarding important CSR skills. In addition, we will look at the key issues and concerns surrounding the CSR and the field of customer service in general.

What is a CSR?

Throughout this book we'll discuss the skills and knowledge required to make a CSR successful. And this is a tall order—because the duties of a CSR position are probably more varied than any other job title.

COMMUNICATING WITH CUSTOMERS

Typically, the CSR answers incoming calls and makes outbound calls in response to inquiries, questions, complaints, orders, and problems. Some CSRs provide service exclusively over the telephone, others meet in person with their customers, and some depend on mail, voicemail, e-mail, or fax for customer communications. The CSR may have responsibility for many assigned accounts, perhaps in a particular geographical area, a specialized market—or, in most situations, simply the next customer who calls. Many CSRs work in call centers where thousands of daily customer calls are timed, measured, and reported on in every conceivable manner.

THE CUSTOMER ORDER

If the CSR handles orders, which is often the case, the customer may call to place an order, check status on an order, expedite an order, or make an inquiry before placing an order. As part of the process of providing service, the CSR may advise and counsel the customer, resolve complex problems, illustrate cost savings, state product benefits, educate the customer about the product and/or service, discuss competitors and competing products, and set the stage for future order opportunities. Eventually, the CSR may write an order worth hundreds or thousands of dollars.

ANATOMY OF THE CSR JOB

While most CSRs work a normal business day, many have responsibilities that require different hours. The work often varies from one customer to the next.

Susan's key accounts are on the West Coast. She often stays late in her New Jersey office to talk with her customers, who are three time zones away. Grant, on the other hand, works at a hospital and spends much of his day explaining billing to patients in the surrounding area and discussing their insurance coverage.

Nora arrives at work and immediately checks her e-mail, fax, and voicemail for overnight messages from Japan. Although Nora speaks fluent Japanese, she seldom talks directly with her customers. Shannon supports the sales reps of her company. She provides follow-up on customer orders and inquiries. She rarely talks with the end-user, but is deeply involved in service via her "internal customers," the sales reps.

Allison works in Technical Support and never issues an order, but in a normal day handles a high volume of customer calls coming in to an 800 number. Her callers have questions about their systems, warranties, and service plans. Richard spends the day on the telephone, too, taking customer orders and answering inquiries. In an average day he will write 40 new orders and talk with 60 or more customers.

Karen is involved in support, as well. She listens to customers closely, does some fact finding, and then determines whether a technician should be dispatched to the customer's place of business. Ashley works at the Help Desk, combining her interest in software with her ability to effectively communicate with customers. Customers call her with questions and problems with their software. She enjoys the problem-solving nature of her job. John works for a parts distributor. He talks with customers most of the day, but spends much of his time checking inventory and trying to get someone to solve the backlog situation.

While all of this is going on, Renee from her Paris office is trying to figure the best time for a conference call with her customers Richard in Melbourne and Akihiro in Tokyo.

THE CSR GOAL: PROVIDE QUALITY SERVICE

The common link between all these CSRs is they are trying to meet the first goal of the CSR job: to give high-quality service to customers. When this goal is met, positive things take place. First, *the customer is satisfied*—and that's the most desirable outcome of all. Next, when customers are satisfied, they do some wonderful things. They continue to do business with your organization and they tell other customers about their satisfaction. This means growth for the organization and added opportunity for the CSR.

Customer satisfaction is the ultimate goal of all customer service organizations. Yet, it is strictly customer defined and therefore can't be controlled by the CSR or anyone else within the organization. What *can* be managed are the CSR activities that lead to customer satisfaction. We'll discuss many of these activities throughout the book.

The Value of Word of Mouth

Studies have shown that when customers become dissatisfied and leave an organization, they typically tell nine other people about their dissatisfaction. Those nine people tell others the same story, and they in turn tell another group of people about it and on and on. Word of mouth is important!

BALANCING JELL-O®

Providing quality service on a consistent basis can be thought of as trying to manage five pounds of Jell-O® with your arms, hands, and body. In short, it's difficult! About the time you feel you're gaining control, something slips. Often it's not anything you can control—maybe the product didn't ship on time or an order wasn't filled correctly. Perhaps the customer isn't satisfied with the new management policy, or "must have" information that isn't available. A host of obstacles can get in the way of providing quality service.

EXERCISING TACT

The CSR is usually the one who must skillfully explain difficulties and delays to the customer. Of course, this explanation must be provided in the most tactful way possible, without pointing the finger at another person or work unit within the CSR's organization. The intelligent CSR never discusses internal problems or confidential information with customers.

THREE ELEMENTS THAT CAN HELP OR HINDER

When customers become dissatisfied with service, surveys tell us that the cause can often be found in one or more of the following areas:

- Management policies
- Structure of service
- Actions of frontline customer service

Ironically, these three elements also contribute to customer satisfaction.

Obviously, the frontline CSR has more to do with creating quality service than do management policies or the structure of the service. It is much easier to create successful management policies and a system or structure for delivering service than it is to provide quality CSR frontline service. However, the more customer-satisfying the policies and structure of customer service are, the less time and energy the CSR will have to spend explaining or even defending them. In Section II we'll discuss these conflicts and inequalities in greater detail.

YOU BET THE JOB IS DEMANDING!

To say that the CSR job is a demanding one is an understatement. You need abilities ranging from strong communications skills to good business judgment. The workload is often heavy and can be stressful and loaded with pressure to perform.

In many customer service organizations, stress is recognized as a major concern. I conducted a survey of CSRs in one particular company to determine training needs. The CSRs were asked to select from a list of nearly 40 different training topics. They were unanimous in selecting stress management as a training topic needed for their group.

There are many different reasons—workload chief among them—for high levels of stress within customer service. In this section we will look closely at the CSR's workload and provide some insight on how to manage it.

Stress

From the Wall Street Journal, *May 14, 1996: "Cigna Corp.'s new stress reduction program encourages workers to take group breaks of up to fifteen minutes. They can stretch, dance, or listen to positive affirmations while instrumental music is played. The pilot program launched this month is especially helpful for customer service workers who get glued to their chairs."*

BALANCING INTERNAL AND EXTERNAL OBLIGATIONS

CSRs provide service to customers, but they also have internal obligations within their organizations. Someone has to be the voice of the customer. When the customer isn't satisfied, the CSR is often the first to know and must then deliver the simple but critical message: *"The customer isn't satisfied!"* throughout the organizations. And as delicate as customer communications often are, try telling the company's management and other employees that the customer isn't satisfied! It requires tact and judgment, because so many are affected by the criticism. Self-empowered CSRs take on that job every day and, in enlightened organizations, criticism is expected. A major role for every CSR is to manage the balance between the customer's interest and the interests of the organization. We'll spend more time on this topic, as well, later in the book.

MANAGING THE WORKLOAD THROUGH COMMITMENT

Not every job requires a strong commitment. Some people go to work, do their job—often without any particular enthusiasm—and then go home. Their performance is average, but it's tolerated in many organizations. In short, the employee lacks commitment but manages to get by.

This kind of performance and mind-set are unacceptable in a customer service environment. To be a successful CSR, you have to care about and be committed to customer service. The moment this commitment weakens, it is reflected in the CSR's performance.

NO COMMITMENT, NO CUSTOMER!

Customers immediately perceive a CSR's lack of interest and poor attitude and will not tolerate it for very long. There's always a competitor who keeps calling and sending information, trying to lure the customer away. If the competitor has similar products, services, and prices, plus a reputation for quality service, they are poised to move in and capture your customer. A sure way to pave the way for your competitors is to show a lack of commitment to your customers.

Though several factors come into play as well, consistent, high-quality customer service can't be delivered unless there is commitment on the CSR's part. A commitment to understand the customer's needs, to maintain effective communication, to seek every reasonable avenue to satisfy the customer, and to do this with every customer conversation—all these are essential. It's a difficult task but it can be done. It begins with commitment.

VALUING THE CUSTOMER

What's most important in your organization? Yes, the quality of your product, service, employees, and management are crucial. But it's the customer that's most important. A customer may do business with you for years and be considered a loyal and dependable buyer of your products or services. Over this period you have provided good service and made every effort to satisfy this customer. Then suddenly this "loyal and dependable customer" is gone. Gone are the orders, shipments, inquiries, problems to solve, and other communication. "How can they do this to us? Look at all we've done for them over the years!" exclaims the manager. "I thought they were ours," says the salesperson. But you don't own your customers; to keep them, you must value them.

CUSTOMERS ARE FREE TO LEAVE ANYTIME

When CSRs, salespeople, and others on your staff start thinking they own a customer, the customer may provide quite a surprise. Free to leave and do business with whomever they want, customers frequently make these "stay or go" decisions based on the quality of the service they receive. That's why *consistent* CSR performance is so critical. The customer's view of the service provided may not extend much beyond the last contact with a CSR, so *every* CSR interaction with the customer is vitally important.

THE EMPLOYER'S EXPECTATION VS. THE CUSTOMER'S NEEDS

To the CSR, employers and managers are a little like customers. They expect a great deal. They want everyone in the company—customer service, the help desk, order processing, inside sales, and other groups— to be responsible for satisfying the customer. It's a reasonable expectation. So the CSR balances both: On one hand there's the customer and on the other is the organization, and it's not always sweet harmony between the two. "Natural conflicts" arise; it's that Jell-O® thing again!

THE CUSTOMER WANTS AN EXPEDITE

Let's look at a typical example of this conflict. A customer makes a strong case for expediting her order. She says the order must be expedited or it will delay the opening of their new offices. CSR, Maury, thinks the request is reasonable and tells the customer, "Let me see what I can do for you." He talks with the Operations, Scheduling, and Production departments and is told, "We can't change the production schedule for one customer, it's too expensive. The customer should have placed the order sooner." Finally Maury goes to his boss and pleads the customer's case. The boss makes a few calls and reports back "It's too late and too expensive to change the production schedule. The customer will have to delay the opening of their new office." Maury reluctantly agrees to report the bad news to the customer.

CSRs are sometimes successful in achieving complete satisfaction for the customers they represent, but at other times they simply cannot. Maury's company made a business decision not to change the production schedule, so how does Maury present it to his customer? He can't say, "I did my best but those fools wouldn't listen. I can't believe what a terrible decision they made." He might want to say that, but his response has to be stated in businesslike terms with as much positive emphasis as possible. Maury's response must relay an attitude that says, "I will represent my customer as best I can, but I will always present my organization in as positive a light as possible." So here's what Maury can say to his customer: "I'm sorry, Ms. Jones, I wasn't able to get our production schedule altered to accommodate your request. The cost to do so would be prohibitive. I know this is not the answer you wanted, but it's the best we can do. Hopefully, we can work more closely together to prevent this type of situation from occurring in the future."

It's another example of balancing the interest of the customer and the organization. Every successful CSR does it, often on a daily basis.

HARD SKILLS VS. SOFT SKILLS

To some managers and other employees, the boundaries of customer service and the CSR position are a little blurred. Customer service doesn't follow the same disciplines within a business as accounting, production, engineering, inventory management, and other units. These departments require *hard skills* that are easier to define and generally less complicated to measure. In contrast, customer service is focused on a combination of *soft* and *hard skills.* The CSR hard skills typically revolve around product knowledge, information systems, procedures, and business policies. The soft skills are focused on customer communications.

Providing quality customer service is not like producing accounting ledgers or creating software. The principles involved are not so pragmatic as those used in engineering or in other technical areas. As a result, there is sometimes a conflict between the soft skill requirements of the CSR position and the hard skill focus of the organization. Let's return to Maury's situation, where the customer wanted an expedite. The production people might be left wondering why a CSR would even ask to change the schedule to satisfy one customer. This is a fairly normal response, because production and operations people generally think in terms of systems, planning, and managing and less in terms of customers. Over at customer service, the reasoning is simple: Maury's customer needed it!

In enlightened organizations, everyone thinks of the customer first, and that means conflicts and differences among the staff are minimized. Even in the most enlightened situation, however, it can be difficult to get individual work units and departments to consistently focus on customer needs.

Technical Support Requires Soft Skills, Too

Many high-tech organizations have technical support groups. Their responsibilities include support of technical products; and answering inquiries and solving problems for end-user customers, resellers, distributors, their own sales force, and others. The job requires considerable technical expertise and often a degree in computer science or the equivalent. Education and training are required to understand systems, computer components, or other high-tech products. To satisfy the customer, technical knowledge is of course a key skill—but the soft skills of customer communication come strongly into play. The message, whether it's technical or basic, must always be delivered in the customer's terms.

THE FINALE: A CUSTOMER-FOCUSED ORGANIZATION

Maury's customer's expedite situation fits nicely into the category of a "natural conflict." When management is customer focused, however, they expect this type of conflict to occur. Why? Because they understand that a successful CSR must represent the customer's interest and make the customer's case. Organizations focused on customer service expect the CSR to be the customer's advocate. They also welcome reminders from the CSR and from others with direct contact with the customer, about the importance of customers. These companies anticipate that CSRs will articulate what the customers want and need. (See Figure 1.)

The Customer-Focused Organization

The Order

The CSR writes an order for 22 widgets and notices there are only six left in inventory. The CSR tells operations "We need more widgets, we may get another order." Operations replies, "Good news, we finally got rid of some of those widgets." Do you think the CSR and operations have two different views of this order?

Balancing the interests of the customer and the organization is an important topic. In Section II, we will explore how developing a professional approach for CSRs contributes to this balance.

II

DEVELOPING PROFESSIONALISM

Because of the importance of customer service, CSR professionalism is a must.

> **Professionalism:** Upholding the highest possible service standards by employing methods, conduct, and qualities that will lead to customer satisfaction.

WHAT ARE YOUR SERVICE STANDARDS?

Every organization has standards for implementing their customer service policy. In customer-focused organizations, these standards often are formal statements of policy or service goals. Customer service standards in such organizations are topics for ongoing discussion.

Unfortunately, in far too many organizations, service standards are happenstance and unclear. As a result, the expectations regarding CSR performance are sometimes equally vague, and attention is only given to them when there are problems.

Whether a company is systematic and organized in its approach to standards, or whether it leaves a lot to chance and circumstance, the fact remains: All business organizations want to produce customer satisfaction. The CSR role in either type of organization is critical and demands *professionalism.* This professionalism may be a byproduct of the corporate culture or may be imposed from management in a top-down fashion. It can also be driven by the CSR. There is no substitute for a CSR who acts in a professional and self-empowered manner.

In this section we will examine the elements of professionalism and illustrate how they can support customer service standards.

CSR EMPOWERMENT

Empowerment has been defined in many different ways. It's been called responsible freedom to satisfy the customer, use of good judgment, and making quality business decisions on behalf of the customer. Really, it's all of these. Although we usually think of empowerment as being handed off from management, it often originates with the CSR in the form of self-empowerment. For the self-empowered CSR, activities are not completely dictated by management. Instead, the CSR motivates himself or herself toward acting empowered.

When management decides the scope of CSR responsibility, the CSR is expected to function within that range. This style of empowerment is often more a form of management control. Management may not intend to restrict the CSR, but in reality, this is what often happens. When CSRs must get their supervisor's approval on routine decisions and actions there will be little empowerment. The more empowerment is defined by rules, regulations, restrictive policies, and procedures, the less empowerment there will be. CSRs, like all employees, want to have a responsible position within the organization. They will accept their responsibility and act in a self-empowered manner if allowed to do so—without the restrictions of authority and responsibility that are too closely defined.

WHY SHOULD THE CSR BE EMPOWERED IN THE FIRST PLACE?

When CSRs are empowered, the result is customer satisfaction. Customers often need maximum representation within the organizations they do business with, and an empowered CSR can provide that representation. In the example considered in Section I, Maury's customer required an expedited order. Maury talked with Operations, Scheduling, Production, and his own boss to try to meet the customer's need. Although he wasn't successful, he represented the customer well.

This CSR acted in an empowered manner. Before he made his request on behalf of the customer, he knew it would be difficult to change the production schedule, but be tried anyway. He made the customer's need clearly known. Organizations must hear what their customers need, and empowered CSRs make that possible.

CUSTOMERS KNOW THE DIFFERENCE

When CSRs are empowered, their customers know it. Ask them. You will get a quick Yes or No. When the answer is Yes, you will also hear comments like "She does a great job for us." "He's very reliable; we can depend on his service." And "She always finds a way to get the job done for us." Customers sense when the CSR is acting on their behalf, even when the results are bad news for the customer, as in our expedite case. In that situation, the customer didn't get what she wanted, but she probably realized the CSR made an empowered effort. She was made to understand that it was a business decision similar to the ones she has to make. Because Ms. Jones has learned to trust her CSR, she knew her CSR would try—because he always gives a maximum effort.

RESPECT THE RULES AND PROCEDURES, BUT BE FLEXIBLE

Empowerment does not mean ignoring or abusing company policies, rules, and procedures. Nor does it mean these rules can't be changed when they interfere with customer service. Policies, rules, and procedures need ongoing review by the customer, the CSR, and others who interact with customers. For an enlightened organization, where the CSR is empowered, this is standard practice. When the organization stands stubbornly behind inflexible policies or rules towards customer service problems usually arise.

No Exceptions = Unhappy Customers

During the busiest hours of the day (11:00 A.M. to 4:00 P.M.), management of one popular credit union decided the CSRs should not make outgoing calls. "No exceptions," the CSRs were told. One result was that more incoming calls got answered. However, it also happened that the CSRs reported considerable customer dissatisfaction: It took too long for customer callbacks to be made. The CSRs were not empowered to make their own decisions about when to make an exception.

In this example, management is trying to better control the in-and-out call volume of customer service. The plan to restrict outgoing calls during peak hours is a common one. Logic dictates, however, that the CSR needs to be empowered to return customer calls when the situation is urgent, or for other important reasons. To take the risk of irritating customers with this type of callback policy is foolish. The CSR can satisfy the management policy most of the time yet be empowered to make an occasional exception.

EMPOWERMENT: A MIND-SET

CSR empowerment is for the most part a mind-set—a fixed mental attitude or disposition that predetermines the CSR's response to customer situations. Empowerment can also be described as an inclination or a habit. Let's look at an example.

Maria from Wafer Inc. calls and requests a rush order for 100 pieces of product. The CSR checks the inventory and finds 200 pieces in stock, but orders are pending for 125 pieces; only 75 are available for shipment. What should the CSR do? It will depend on her mind-set. A reactive CSR might tell Maria, "I have 75 that I'll ship immediately, and 25 will be on back order." Another CSR who has a blame-placing mind-set might tell the customer that "Purchasing is responsible for the lack of product." In contrast, the CSR with a creative and proactive mind-set will determine when the pending orders are due and if there are inventory replacement orders pending. This CSR will then try to make a deal with another CSR to borrow 25 pieces of product. If that doesn't work, this CSR with a problem-solving mind-set will find another solution.

In their book, *Empowerment,* authors Cynthia Scott and Dennis Jaffe discuss the mind-set shift an employee must experience to act empowered: "Some of these shifts involve a drastic re-orientation of the way we see our work." Using some of the Scott/Jaffe model, we can describe an empowered CSR by showing the required mind-set shift a CSR must experience.

The following chart illustrates a mind-set shift from negative to positive. Use the 1 to 5 rating scale to grade your present mind-set status for each topic on the chart. If, for example, you feel and act strongly empowered as a CSR give yourself a 4 or 5 in the category.

MIND-SETS

FROM	TO	SELF RATING (CIRCLE ONE)				
Powerless—Afraid to act independently	*Empowered*—Takes action	1	2	3	4	5
Waiting for instructions—From the boss or others	*Taking action*—Stepping forward to satisfy the customer	1	2	3	4	5
Doing things right—Never deviating from the rules, regulations, and policies	*Doing the right thing*—Making the right decision for the customer	1	2	3	4	5
Reactive—Taking action only in response to the customer	*Creative and proactive*—Making the right decision for the customer	1	2	3	4	5
Someone else is responsible—"It's not my fault."; "I can't change the way we do things."	*Personally responsible*—"I accept responsibility."	1	2	3	4	5
Blame placing—"It's Production's fault!" (or Accounting, or Marketing, or Management)	*Problem solving*—"I'll be part of the solution."	1	2	3	4	5
Reluctance—To act empowered. To help the customer.	*Willingness*—To act empowered. To help the customer.	1	2	3	4	5
No ownership—Of the customer's problem	*Taking ownership*—"If the customer has a problem, then I have a problem."	1	2	3	4	5
Giving up—"What's the use?"; "I can't change anything."	*Persistence*—"I'll keep on trying."	1	2	3	4	5
Lack of customer focus—Focused internally	*Always focused on the customer*	1	2	3	4	5

Now that you've rated yourself, where do you stand? Every CSR needs to measure his or her mind-set. Ask yourself three questions.

- To what extent have I moved towards a customer-focused mind-set?

- What is my progress to date?

- What do I need to do to improve my mind-set?

The 1 to 5 ratings provide considerable insight into individual mind-sets and will illustrate where improvement is needed.

INTERNAL APPLICATION OF SELF-EMPOWERMENT: TEAMWORK

We normally think of empowerment in relationship to how the CSR interacts with the customer, but there are opportunities to act empowered within an organization as well. This is especially true in the area of teamwork and contributing as a team member. Assuming personal responsibility for the promotion and execution of teamwork is a must for every member of the CSR team. When the CSR is a member of a team, it's an opportunity to contribute to the success of that team by playing an active role.

Teamwork doesn't run on it own power; it requires the players to push, shove, and pull it along. It needs promotion, or it will first diminish and then disappear. The self-empowered CSR team can maintain and grow the team process using the following ideas.

SIX WAYS FOR THE CSR TO PROMOTE TEAMWORK

1. Encourage others to be team players.
   - Present a positive example.
   - Emphasize the team approach.

2. Take responsibility for teamwork.

- Get involved and contribute to the team.

- Promote the team concept as the "solution."

- Encourage others to step up to more responsibility.

3. Readily share your knowledge and new information.

4. Strive to make the team successful.

- Stay positive.

- Minimize the "drama."

- Encourage problem solving and conflict resolution through the team process.

5. Remain open to new and different ideas.

- Encourage openness during team discussions.

- Listen to others and show respect for their ideas.

6. Keep in mind that teamwork doesn't always function perfectly.

- Be willing to try.

- Continue to try.

Imagine a team or work unit where these six ideas were part of the everyday environment. Wouldn't that be a wonderful place to work? Help make your organization one of those places.

The Balancing Act

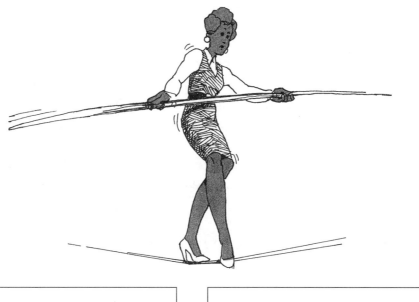

Customer Interests and Responsibilities	Organizational Interests and Responsibilities

EXERCISING JUDGMENT

As first mentioned in Section I, balancing a customer's interests with those of your organization is an important part of CSR professionalism. When the CSR's organization is strongly customer focused, there's not much risk associated with representing customer needs. In fact, it's expected.

But to be successful, a CSR needs to understand when to push for the customer, how far to go with the effort, and when to back off. It's a matter of *exercising good judgment.* Let's look at two examples of CSR judgment: Karen and Sean.

Karen Pushes Too Hard

Karen provides service for several large accounts. One of the customers asked for 60-day payment terms instead of the usual 30 days, because of "temporary cash flow problems." Karen called Accounting and asked for the arrangement, but found out this customer had been paying their invoices in 45 days, not 30. They were always late and their financial situation "didn't look favorable." Accounting said they couldn't provide the extra days. Karen then called the Accounting manager and got the same answer. Next, she went to her boss for help. He told her to politely tell the customer "No." Karen decided to call the VP of Finance, who also turned her down. When Karen's boss became very upset with her and questioned her judgment, Karen said, "I'm just trying to represent the customer."

Why has Karen's judgment been called into question? Because she continued to look for an unrealistic answer to the customer's situation. Because of the customer's payment record and unfavorable financial situation, there was little probability of meeting the request. It was *not in the best interest of the organization.* Karen should have realized this early on and given her customer a polite refusal.

Let's look at another example. This time, the CSR successfully balances the customer's interests with that of the organization.

Sean Makes a Trade Off

One of Sean's most significant and profitable accounts called and ordered 25 units of 712 components. Sean knew the customer's time frame couldn't be met using the 712s, so he recommended substituting the new 714s. The customer agreed to the replacement, but didn't want to pay the difference of $10 in the price of the 714s. Sean made a judgment call; he discounted the 714 components to the 712 price. He told his boss what he had done, and she agreed with his decision. He sent a fax to Accounting explaining the billing arrangement. Accounting called Sean's boss and received authorization for the discount.

Sean felt empowered to offer the price discount *because it was in the best interest of both his organization and the customer to meet the time frame.* In addition, he included his boss in the decision-making process, because he knew Accounting would call her. Sean's example illustrates successful balancing.

Another consideration is that Sean was offering the discount to a large account. For a less significant account, Sean is probably not empowered to offer a discount because it's not in the best interest of the organization. A $250.00 discount on a large order will easily be made up with future orders. It's in the organization's best interest to make certain the major accounts, which contribute more to profits, are satisfied.

GOOD JUDGMENT IS A SKILL LIKE ANY OTHER

Exercising good judgment is a skill that can mean success or failure for the CSR. The more empowerment the CSR assumes, the more individual judgment becomes critical. Advancement in the CSR ranks depends on many different factors, but good judgment is at the top of most lists. When a CSR demonstrates good judgment it's appreciated on two fronts—by the organization and by the customer. Why? Because both have someone they can trust with decisions.

Lisa Has a Decision to Make

Lisa's customer will be on vacation during the week when a special-order paper is due to arrive. The customer tells her, "When it comes in, go ahead and ship it. If it doesn't get here, we'll take what you have in stock and pay the higher price. We have to get the project started and the paper is critical."

The less-expensive paper arrives on time. Lisa knows the profit margin on the paper in stock is considerably higher, and her company wants to sell as much of it as possible. What should she do? Which paper does she ship? Which paper does her organization want shipped? In this situation, what's the best way to balance the customer's and the paper company's interests? What would you do?

Certainly Lisa could ship the higher-priced paper, but good judgment and a little basic honesty dictate that she doesn't. Her company's interests are well served by providing the best service at the best price for the customer.

GOOD JUDGMENT MEANS GOOD BALANCE

One indicator of the importance of quality judgment is the impact CSR decisions have on both the customer and the organization. Determining the right balance is critical. Remember Karen? She pursued the customer's interest to an extreme by continually asking those in authority to make what seemed to be an unwise business decision. In each of Lisa's and Sean's decisions, on the other hand, there was balance.

When you are confronted with making a decision about the best path to follow, ask yourself these questions. They will help any CSR exercise good judgment and achieve a balance between the customer's and the organization's interests.

Questions that Measure CSR Judgment

- Does my decision make good business sense?

- How well does my decision balance the customer's and my organization's interest?

- Are there alternative decisions that should be considered?

CAREER TIP: CSRs can gain either a positive or negative reputation within their organization by the way they represent the customer's interest. As they interact and negotiate with other departments or work units, CSRs have opportunities to demonstrate a variety of skills—ranging from simple tact to the ability to negotiate on behalf of the customer. How well these opportunities are managed by the CSR is noticed throughout the organization. In trying to help your customer, if you come on too strong and demonstrate little tact, you'll earn a poor reputation. On the other hand, if you demonstrate tact and good judgment, you'll gain a strong reputation for balancing customer and organizational interest—important to any CSR's career.

CSR SELF-MANAGEMENT

Successful CSRs are good self-managers. In any type of managing, the way to reach a goal is to control the activities leading up to it. As stated earlier, the CSR's chief goal is to provide quality service and, in the process, enjoy a rewarding job. To achieve this goal, a variety of activities come into play. Foremost is the critical activity of self-managing the responsibilities of the job. Let's closely examine one of these important responsibilities—the CSR's workload.

MANAGING THE CSR

The CSR's workload is usually heavy in volume. Customer demands vary, and there are periods of time when the phones never quit ringing. New policies, procedures, services, and products come along that must be learned, and this means time-consuming meetings and training sessions. Take a few hours away from the desk, and the workload increases even more. The number of CSRs is not always equal to the organization's workload. This understaffing—caused by increased customer demand, business growth, CSR turnover, and other factors—often dramatically increases individual workloads. It's important to keep in mind that the CSR job is for those who want a fast-paced, challenging, and rewarding environment. An absolute requirement is the ability to adapt to a changing workload.

CUSTOMER SERVICE IS DIFFERENT

The CSR isn't the only worker who has a demanding, dynamic workload. However, more than most jobs, the CSR position is in a constant state of flux. Often, during some sort of change or growth period, the CSR workload is the first to be affected—seemingly overnight. New products and services are introduced and the workload gets even heavier. A change in management policy may suddenly produce a few hundred additional calls. Customer demand is hard to predict, but management typically has to see evidence of the demand before they are willing to hire and train new CSRs. Guess who handles the extra work in the meantime?

CHANGES IN THE BUSINESS ENVIRONMENT

Adding to the dynamic nature of customer service are the changes that normally occur in the general business environment. Reorganization and downsizing are two common examples. When business slows, customer service may quickly be perceived as overstaffed. What has been an unstoppable demand for your product can quickly change.

FOUR STEPS FOR HANDLING YOUR WORKLOAD

CSRs, like all employees, need to be flexible and possess a willingness to meet the new challenges that change brings about. Flexibility and a willingness to grow and adapt are essential requirements. Here are four steps you can take toward successfully managing the CSR workload:

1. Establish priorities

2. Manage your time well

3. Be proactive

4. Keep a positive attitude

NOTE: Section IV of this book offers a self-improvement program to help you develop your ability to execute these steps.

STEP 1: ESTABLISH PRIORITIES

The CSR must learn to identify and establish the priorities of the job—today and over the long term as well.

WHAT YOU CAN DO NOW

In the short term, in daily or weekly activities, many CSRs simply create a "things to do" list and then prioritize that list. This lets you provide order and logic to the tasks at hand. The tasks can be categorized as follows:

- Must do
- Should do
- Would like to do

The daily emphasis is, of course, on the "must do" and "should do" items.

WHAT YOU CAN DO FOR THE LONG TERM

Establishing daily or weekly priorities will help you in managing the immediate workload. To gain more control and for increased productivity, long-term activities need to come into focus as well. Begin by setting long-term objectives. These objectives may be your own, or may be imposed by the organization. In either case, they should be designed to improve your ability to manage daily activities. Here are a few examples of typical long-term CSR objectives.

A. Objective:	Improve product/service knowledge	
Benefits:	Easier to explain products/service	
	Improved customer service	
	Faster call handling	
	Increased average value or size of order	

B. Objective: Become more proficient in completing order-entry work

  Benefits: Save time and improve accuracy

Reduce the organization's expense

C. Objective: Improve customer communications skills

  Benefits: Better job management

More customer satisfaction

D. Objective: Create stronger relationships with other work units

  Benefits: More cooperation among departments in serving the customer

Improved teamwork

Establish activities that will support your objectives. For example, to improve customer communications skills, the activities might involve additional training, reading, observing and talking with other CSRs, viewing training videos, and a host of other activities. Next, establish a timeline for completion of the activities. The result: a basic but effective self-improvement program.

STEP 2: MANAGE YOUR TIME WELL

Establishing priorities and objectives is meaningless unless you know how to manage the time available to implement them. Every CSR needs a time-management system. Volumes have already been written on the subject, because managing time is an absolute necessity for success. Some people seem to manage their time easily and naturally, but most of us struggle with this concept, letting events and people control our time. We end up wasting time, which reduces our productivity.

Author Marion E. Haynes, in his excellent book *Personal Time Management,* describes common time wasters: disorganization, procrastination, attitude, gossiping, unnecessary perfectionism, unproductive meetings, and several other factors which contribute to the problem of wasting time. A good way for the CSR to begin a program for improved time management is to identify personal time-wasters.

Brett's Personal Time-Wasters

Brett believed there was simply not enough time in the day for him to get his job done. He often came in early and stayed late to complete his work. When he complained, his boss suggested that he was "wasting a great deal of time on most days." Brett was upset by his boss's comment but decided to be positive and try to identify his "time-wasters." For a two-week period, he tracked every minute of his time. He was surprised to learn that playing telephone tag accounted for nearly 45 minutes every day. He determined that by using e-mail more frequently and leaving additional information on voicemail, he could save nearly 30 minutes a day. Brett also found he could shorten his team meetings by taking on more responsibility for the organization and success of the meetings he attended. Finally, Brett learned that his social time at work was consuming at least 45 minutes per day. He decided to reduce it by 50%.

Recovering even a few hours a week will probably mean that you don't have to work late or come in early quite as often. The following basic formula for improving productivity will work for all of us.

Formula to Improve Productivity

Recovering time + Reemployment of that time = Improved productivity

Identifying your time-wasters is a good beginning for most CSRs. To become an effective manager of your time, you may need to do some study and research to find a method or system that works for you. Check your library for books on time management. Ask a successful CSR or coworker how they manage time. At a team meeting, introduce time management as a discussion topic. In managing your personal time, be willing to change what isn't working. Strive to develop a system that works for you.

STEP 3: BE PROACTIVE AND LESS REACTIVE

Most CSRs are controlled by customer calls. The typical CSR comes to work, the phone starts ringing, and the activity begins. The demand for customer service is all encompassing; it drives nearly all CSR activity. You may find it almost impossible to plan much of the day beyond answering customer calls, entering orders, answering inquiries, and managing other CSR responsibilities.

Today many organizations want the CSR to be more proactive, more on top of things, and less reactive. More than one CSR has thought management has "gone too far" in making these suggestions about becoming more proactive. The immediate response is often "How can I become proactive when I'm controlled by the customer call?" It's a valid question, and one we can answer by first defining the term proactive:

> **Proactive:** Acting in advance to deal with an expected event or difficulty.

THE PROACTIVE MIND-SET

Try to develop a proactive mind-set. This means you are focused on taking responsibility, on acting rather than reacting. Instead of feeling powerless over your work situation, you become and can act empowered. Don't wait for orders; take action, instead. Accept personal responsibility for customer satisfaction. Solve your customer problems rather than placing blame on others. In short, be a creative "can-do" person.

BEING READY FOR YOUR CUSTOMER CALLS

Since the customer call is all-important to the CSR, this seems to be the logical place to start being proactive. *Being proactive can center around acting in advance of the expected customer call.*

For most CSRs, their customer calls control the day's activities. The most common difficulty that comes up is a customer situation that is critical— for example, the satisfaction of a key customer. These key customers often have requests and inquiries that must be satisfied within specific time frames. Let's see how you can become more proactive and actually get ahead of the next customer call.

Reactive Randy

Randy manages a large number of calls per day. He typically runs behind schedule throughout most of the day and often says, "There are times when I can't catch up." Randy's situation is somewhat typical of many CSRs, but more often than not there's a way to regain some time and reduce the number of incoming calls. For example, Randy may be able to change a percentage of his incoming calls to outgoing calls. What's the difference? He still has the same number of calls, but Randy gains more control because he determines when the call is made.

Calling customers on a proactive basis is typically better customer service. The following is a plan for Randy to become more proactive in his customer calls, and it can work for you, too.

THE PROACTIVE CUSTOMER CALL PLAN WORKSHEET

1. Review all customer calls over a five-day period.   _____
   (Randy had 150 calls.)

2. Identify the percentage of incoming vs. outgoing   _____
   customer calls.
   (Randy has 120 incoming [80%] and 30 outgoing [20%]).

3. Identify the number of repeat calls.   _____
   (Randy had 8 customers who made a second call
   because he wasn't able to get back to them within
   their time frame.)

4. Identify the number of "expected" customer calls.   _____
   (Randy has 10 customers that he knew from the
   beginning of the week would call.)

5. Identify the number of individual customers who call   _____
   every week.
   (Randy has 3.)

Add Items 3, 4, and 5 to get the number of possible outgoing calls.

Total Items 3, 4, and 5   _____

Randy's customer call survey results are fairly straightforward. He had 21 calls (the total of items 3, 4, and 5) that potentially could be outbound rather than incoming calls. By making timely calls to a majority of these customers, Randy has the opportunity to be proactive. He gains more control of his workload, time schedule, and, of course, improves service to his customers.

OTHER WAYS TO BE PROACTIVE

Being proactive will not only help you manage your workload, but also will increase customer satisfaction. In addition to anticipating and making outbound customer calls on time, there are other proactive customer activities that you can undertake. For example, work on improving product knowledge. It will allow you to answer nearly all questions on the first call, thereby avoiding customer callbacks. Sending out new product or service information as it becomes available is a good way to be proactive, rather than waiting for the customer to make a request. By learning more about the customer's business, you can eliminate routine repetitive questions.

Of course, each CSR job is different; consequently, the opportunities for becoming more proactive will vary. Without a doubt, however, the more knowledge you have of your customers, the easier it becomes to identify these opportunities. Remaining in the reactive mode means average performance; becoming proactive moves you to a higher level.

STEP 4: KEEP A POSITIVE ATTITUDE

It's often been said that you need two things to work successfully in a customer service environment. You need a great attitude, and a sense of humor. CSRs who provide quality service over the long haul invariably have both.

Like the subject of time management, a great deal has been written about positive attitudes, and it's worth a trip to the library to read about the techniques others use to stay on the positive track. In this section, we'll study one particular concept that is an absolute key to maintaining a positive attitude: choice.

ATTITUDE IS A CHOICE

Attitude is a choice—even in the midst of a hectic and chaotic customer service environment. Successful people have positive attitudes, and successful CSRs are no exception. This is not to say your positive attitude won't be challenged, because it will be. To decide to be positive and to remain constantly in a positive state is nearly impossible. What you must do, in effect, is to choose a positive attitude again and again. It's a repetitive process that may occur several times a day.

For some, these choices may be made without much conscious thought. For others, when their positive attitude is challenged, the choice must be made consciously and specifically. But once we learn that our attitude will be challenged by people, places, and things, we can learn to recognize the situation and then choose to remain positive.

Let's say you've received three consecutive calls from three different upset customers. One customer's shipment didn't arrive as promised. Another customer's invoice is wrong—again. Yet another customer is threatening to cancel his account because of poor service he received.

Momentarily, you are overwhelmed, just as most of us would be. This is exactly the point where choice comes into play. For most, these negative experiences make it difficult to remain positive. In fact, feeling "down" and at least a little negative is pretty normal behavior. But, there's work to do and more customers who need service. A conscious, positive attitude choice has to be made. The payoff is guaranteed—your consistent and conscious effort to be positive will produce the results you want.

BEWARE OF THE DRAMA

When change is brought about by growth or other factors and workloads increase as a result, attitudes can easily suffer. Let's see what happens in Curt's case.

Curt's Dilemma

Curt's company was growing rapidly. Nearly every work group, but especially customer service, was feeling the strain. Even as Curt worked harder and put in extra hours, he could feel his normal positive attitude slipping away. He was angry at his company for not adding new CSRs fast enough. He knew the workloads could get back to normal with just a few new people contributing. Instead, many of his customers were experiencing delays, and this made them more difficult to deal with. Curt could feel the added stress. He was leaving work nearly every day disappointed and frustrated. Curt could see that other CSRs had the same poor attitude. He wanted to act to change the situation but wasn't sure what to do.

What happens next in a situation like Curt's is called "the drama." In fact, many of you will recognize it as a situation you have personally experienced. There is a discussion, gossip, confusion, and other talk that is basically unproductive. The topics are what the organization is doing, what it isn't doing, what it may do, and of course what it should do. This drama is something the knowledgeable CSR will simply avoid— because it's unproductive, a major time-waster, and has a negative impact on everyone's attitude. You can participate, or you can choose to remain positive and work constructively for improvement. It's almost that simple. Selecting the positive path allows a CSR to stay focused on the objective at hand: customer satisfaction.

AN EFFECTIVE PLAN TO REMAIN POSITIVE

Here are five ideas that form a strong plan to make sure you make the right attitude choice.

1. Be conscious of the attitude you display.
   - Are you positive toward customers and coworkers alike?
   - Do you use positive language, emphasizing to the customer what you *can* do rather than what you *can't* do?
   - Listen to yourself. Are you hearing positive things?

2. Keep your self-talk positive.
   - Frame your internal thoughts in positive terms.
   - Push yourself to think and act in a positive manner.

3. Associate with the positive people in your life.
   - Why spend your lunch period with a negative coworker?
   - Hang around with your "positive" coworkers.

4. Choose to be a positive force within your work group.
   - Be a positive role model for the rest of the group.
   - Find the positive attributes of coworkers.
   - Avoid office drama and gossip.
   - Try to diffuse negative office situations.

5. Make the decision and the choice to be positive.
   - Turn adversity into a challenge to be positive.
   - Share your positive thoughts and ideas.

How do you rate your attitude on a 1-to-10 scale? Are you satisfied with your rating?

THE PERSONAL ENERGY QUESTION

A high energy level is essential to work in a fast-paced customer service environment. A negative attitude will drain most people emotionally and definitely impair performance. Conversely, a positive attitude builds energy and can gather momentum as it grows. Watch a coworker who has a high energy level, and you will generally find a positive attitude as well. It's hard to be and act energized without having positive feelings.

THE CUSTOMER NOTICES

One final comment regarding a positive attitude. Keep in mind that a positive attitude will help you manage even the most demanding workload, and it's also something customers expect. Your customer knows within the first few moments of a conversation whether your frame of mind is positive or negative. Your tone of voice, what you say, how you say it—all the factors involved in a conversation will be quickly and usually, expertly read. Customers want to work with positive CSRs and instinctively know when that's not the case.

MANAGING THE TECHNOLOGY

The technology available to aid the career of a CSR must be managed in order to have its best effect. CSRs have at their command a variety of tools, ranging from the telephone itself to voicemail, e-mail, conference calling, and fax. Each of these tools is designed to enhance communication, but you need skill and knowledge to utilize them successfully. To manage this technology means to use it correctly, carefully, and with good judgment.

FAXES

Mike Sends the Wrong Message

As a CSR, Mike is careful of how he speaks to his customers. One of his customers calls and reduces a pending order for workstation equipment, explaining that the reason for the reduced order was "possible layoffs." Mike changes the order, and on the cover sheet of the fax confirming the changes, he writes "Sorry to hear about your layoffs."

Mike has demonstrated an incredible lack of good judgment. He either wasn't thinking or believes that a fax is some sort of private communication. Fax machines are nearly always general office equipment, and there is very little about them that's private.

With this in mind, fax messages should be considered formal business documents and should be formatted with care and with the realization that people other than the disignated recipients may read them. CSRs should take the same care in sending a fax they would take in writing a standard business letter.

E-MAIL ONLY SEEMS SIMPLE

There's an interesting and well-written book titled *The 3 Rs of E-Mail: Risks, Rights, and Responsibilities* by Hartman and Nantz. The authors emphasize the need for good judgment and knowledge of proper e-mail procedures and guidelines. E-mail is meant to be, and usually is, faster and cheaper than other forms of communication. But, as the authors point out, that's not always the case. E-mail addresses often get way too much personal mail and assorted trivia, to the point that important messages may be overlooked.

E-mail is not without problems and concerns. Here are five rules to consider when sending a customer an e-mail message:

- Don't assume the message is private.

- Keep the message short and businesslike.

- Clearly state the purpose of your message.

- Find out if the customer reads e-mail regularly.

- When in doubt, ask.

CONFERENCE CALLING

For CSRs and their customers, conference calls are typical avenues for resolving customer issues. Here are basic but important guidelines to follow during these conference calls.

- When a customer is part of the conference call, make certain that any coworkers who are participating know that the customer is on the line.

- Use even more discretion than normal because of the number of people involved.

- When speakerphones are in use, remember, you don't know who may be listening. Be careful.

- When you use a speakerphone during a customer conversation, be certain the customer knows it.

VOICEMAIL

What do you suppose the world was like before voicemail? Did people actually answer their own telephones? Have you ever wondered if voicemail menus are purposely designed as endless loops?

Voicemail must be managed. If your system asks customers to leave voicemail messages, that system and its procedures must be user friendly. The CSR needs to understand what the customer experiences when they call. Are there voicemail obstacles in the customer's path? Are the customer's voicemail rights being honored? Is the customer satisfied with how your voicemail system is set up? Has anyone asked the customers what they think? Make certain your system satisfies the customer overall, and isn't a major irritant instead.

Voicemail Rights for Customers

Every customer service organization should consider establishing a policy regarding their customers' voicemail rights. Does your organization have one? The following list of voicemail rights are deserved and desired by all customers.

Customer Right #1.   When the CSR is unavailable, I get a choice of leaving a message either in or out of the voicemail system.

Customer Right #2.   When I reach the CSR's voicemail, I will find out when I can reasonably expect a callback.

Customer Right #3.   If I can't wait for a callback, someone will be available at an alternate extension who can help me (not just take a message).

Customer Right #4.   When the CSR leaves a message for me, it will include suggestions for a good time to call back.

Customer Right #5.   A high percentage of the time, the CSR will answer the telephone personally.

Do you think this list of customer voicemail rights is fair? If you were the customer and everything else was about equal in two different companies, but one company honored this set of customer rights, which one would you do business with?

SELF-MANAGEMENT

Let's conclude this section about CSR professionalism with a discussion of managing ourselves as CSRs. One reason CSRs are attracted to customer service is that they like working with people. Another is that they enjoy the autonomous action associated with the job. For example, many customer calls may have similarities, but each customer is different. Satisfying different customers requires skill, versatility, and creativity.

STAY ON YOUR TOES

Although many organizations do considerable training and even designate a structure for the responses they want their customers to hear, not every response and action can be planned in advance. Customer problems and conflicts occur spontaneously, and creativity is often required to solve them. The CSR, more so than others, has to decide on the best course to follow.

GROOMING, DRESS, AND OTHER UNMENTIONABLES

Successful CSR self-management includes being professionally groomed and dressed. You are responsible for presenting a professional image, even when you aren't in a face-to-face meeting with your customer. Just because the CSR's work is centered around the telephone and out of the customer's sight is no excuse for maintaining a less-than-professional appearance. Employers may or may not have written guidelines for grooming and business attire, but their expectation is that the CSR will always be well groomed and properly attired. Walk through the offices of any corporation or organization, and the grooming and dress standards are apparent.

As a CSR, if you have questions about grooming and dress, look around and see how the managers and other leaders look. These staff members typically set the standard. Here are some additional guidelines:

- *Hair:* Clean and neatly combed.
- *Beards and Mustaches:* Neatly trimmed.
- *Clothing:* Clean, not excessive in style, tasteful, in keeping with organization standards.
- *Shoes:* Clean and, if appropriate, polished.
- *Personal Hygiene:* Greasy hair, body odor, bad breath, and dirty nails are unacceptable. (Remember—most of the time, no one will tell you if there's a problem.)

Sloppiness in your grooming and dress will detract from your image faster than almost anything. They are so important that they can easily overshadow the quality work of any CSR. Don't let it happen to you.

SUMMARY: 10 CSR SELF-MANAGEMENT PRINCIPLES

In these past few sections we have discussed several ways CSRs can be strong self-managers. Overall, there are 10 basic principles for CSR self-management. These principles come with a guarantee; employ them consistently and you will become an even stronger self-manager, contributing even more to your potential for success.

CSR Principle #1:   Act in an ethical manner toward the customer and the organization.

CSR Principle #2:   Act with self-empowerment, exercising quality judgment on behalf of the customer and the organization.

CSR Principle #3:   Thoroughly understand the systems, procedures, products, services, and policies of your organization.

CSR Principle #4:   Take responsibility for satisfying the customer.

CSR Principle #5:   When negotiating on behalf of the customer, create win/win situations with coworkers.

CSR Principle #6:   Be committed to your organization, your customer, and your career. Be a role model for others.

CSR Principle #7:   Continually evaluate your personal job skills. Be willing to improve and grow.

CSR Principle #8:   Maintain a positive attitude toward customers and your organization.

CSR Principle #9:   Contribute to teamwork within your organization.

CSR Principle #10:   Help your organization improve its standard of customer service.

III

THE IMPORTANCE OF KNOWING YOUR CUSTOMER

A wise person once said, "To provide quality service that will produce customer satisfaction, you must understand the customer." To understand the customer means to comprehend their expectations and needs. When the customer's expectation and needs are met, customer satisfaction follows. It can also be said, in most situations anyway, that if you meet *most* of the customer's needs and expectations, the customer will also be satisfied. Sounds pretty basic doesn't it? It is! However, it's not that easy to do.

MEETING CUSTOMER EXPECTATIONS

Before discussing how to understand and meet customer expectations, let's define the term.

> ***Customer Expectation:*** Your customer's anticipated value of and level of satisfaction with your service.

EXPECTATIONS CHANGE

Expectations will be different for each situation the customer encounters. For example, imagine you are shopping at your favorite department store, which is having a 30% Off sale for just one day. You have experienced this type of sale before, so a summary of your expectations might be:

- I am going to save money.
- The store will be crowded.
- There will be delays at the point of sale.
- The merchandise will sell fast.
- I will have to go early to have the best selection.
- The store may run out of certain items.
- Service will be slower than normal because the clerks will be busy.
- Parking will be a problem.
- Sale merchandise cannot be returned.

So you go to the sale and experience all of the above expectations, you purchase a few needed items, and you save $70.00. Your greatest expectation, to save money, was realized. You knew from past store sales that your expectation for lack of service would also be realized, but you accepted that without complaint because of the money saved.

The retail store sale situation is similar to commodity purchasing. Commodity sellers don't, or are unable to, add value to the sale; therefore, the customer buys "on price." The customer's perception is that all products and sellers are the same, and for that reason price is the only difference. The customer doesn't see service as a factor.

Let's turn the situation around. Suppose your favorite store is not having a sale but you are going shopping anyway. Your expectations change to the following:

- Prices will be fair.

- Sales clerks will be available and helpful.

- I will have a wide selection of merchandise.

- There will probably be no out-of-stock situations.

- The store will not be crowded.

- There will be no delays.

- I will have access to ample parking.

Now the store, in order to satisfy you, must meet your new expectations. Suppose you go to the store and experience no-return sales conditions, but there are no price reductions. Are you going to be a satisfied customer? Probably not.

The moral of our story? Keep in mind that customer satisfaction is closely tied to meeting customer expectations.

BASIC EXPECTATIONS

Customer expectations change based on where the customer is doing business. One's expectation when calling or meeting with you may be completely different from what that customer anticipates elsewhere. Regardless of the size or type of organization, every customer will have some basic expectations: common courtesy, product or service knowledge, reasonable response time, fair pricing, and honesty. To provide a minimum level of service, these expectations must be met.

Are there other basic customer expectations that apply to your business or job?

_____

_____

_____

When an organization provides a quality product or service along with these basic customer expectations, the odds of success are good. This happens partly because many organizations simply do not meet basic customer expectations. Of course, many others do—organizations such as American Express, IBM, Nordstrom, LifeScan, LensCrafters, Hewlett-Packard, UPS, and countless others meet and exceed these expectations, and are very successful because of it. Does your organization meet these basic but all important customer expectations? As a CSR do you strive to meet them as well?

WHAT DO YOUR CUSTOMERS EXPECT?

Take a moment and make a list of what you think your customers expect. Be sure to include the applicable basic expectations from the preceding section.

_____

_____

_____

TIP: Once you develop your list, bring it to your next team or group meeting. Customer expectation is a good discussion topic for any customer service group. Compare your list of expectations with coworkers' lists, and discuss how to best satisfy your customers.

UNDERSTANDING VARIOUS CUSTOMER STYLES

It hardly needs to be said that each customer is different. As we have discussed, however, their service expectations are usually similar. Just as we did for a few basic expectations, we can also summarize customer behavioral traits, or so-called personality styles. Although each customer is unique, common behavioral patterns consistently appear. One pattern is usually dominant, but the others can also come into play depending on the customer's versatility.

Successful training organizations such as Carlson Learning, Wilson Learning, and others have developed accurate and complete behavioral/personality profile systems. Each of these systems identifies behavior models into which people and customers fall, and instruct people on how to work with these behaviors. This training increases one's understanding of self, customers, coworkers, managers, and others—and, of course, it results in increased customer satisfaction.

Behavior patterns are generally related to the customer's level of assertiveness, the need for details and accuracy, friendliness, and cooperative tendencies. All people have these behavioral tendencies but in different intensities. For example, one customer might display assertiveness by insisting upon a particular service, while demanding considerable detail on how the CSR is going to meet the request. Another customer will be clearly cooperative and friendly, believing that by working together most problems can be solved.

When the CSR is able to recognize the customer's behavioral style, a more satisfactory response can be formulated. Each customer is motivated differently and expects a different response from the CSR. Let's look at three different behavioral patterns and study how to recognize each one and more closely understand the related needs.

THE ASSERTIVE CUSTOMER

Assertive people are often the most difficult for CSRs to deal with. The first problem is that their assertiveness may be strong enough to be interpreted as anger. To the inexperienced CSR, the customer seems angry, perhaps even irate about something or somebody. The reality is that the customer is just being his or her normal, everyday, assertive self. Don't confuse assertive behavior and a direct approach with anger. For example, you may hear assertive statements like the following:

> *"I want this fixed now!"*
>
> *"I can't wait."*
>
> *"The date is unacceptable."*
>
> *"Let me speak to your supervisor."*
>
> *"I don't need to know how and why, just when."*

These statements may even seem aggressive if the customer speaks quickly. But unless you know there is a reason for anger, or the statements and responses are truly harsh, there is no reason to assume the customer is angry.

ASSERTIVE CUSTOMER TRAITS

Whether in person or on the telephone, assertive customers have certain behavioral traits that are easily recognizable. Once the CSR is accustomed to hearing these traits, an appropriate response can be formulated. We have already mentioned two: directness and a faster rate of speech.

Being direct in speech and manner means getting right to the point with little or no unrelated conversation. A highly assertive customer, for example, is not going to talk about the weather or the weekend or much of anything else that's not related to business. He or she is simply going to get down to business. Assertive people are focused on the business itself, not the relationship side of business, on results, not people. They like a fast response, usually with few details. They prefer a faster pace in general. When in positions of authority, their assertive nature may offend others, especially those who are less assertive. More so than other customers, assertive customers understand Yes and No answers. For example, a highly assertive customer may ask for a service or make another request that is difficult to provide, yet will completely understand when the request is denied. With some customers, a CSR may have to explain the "why" of the situation. With an assertive customer, a simple "I'm sorry, we don't provide that service" is often enough.

So, in summary we can say that assertive customer traits are as follows:

- Directness—brief and to the point
- Faster rate of speech
- Focused on business, rather than on relationships and people
- Results-oriented
- Want a fast pace
- Usually don't want many details
- Want control, action, and results

A CONVERSATION WITH AN ASSERTIVE CUSTOMER

The best response for a CSR is to partially mirror the assertive customer. For example, we know the assertive customer wants a fast response. So you can deliver the response briefly and to the point. If you are accustomed to speaking slowly, try to speak a little faster. In short, work toward becoming a little more assertive in your manner, in order to more closely align with the customer.

Here's an example: Suppose the customer has a delivery date that you are not going to be able to meet. It's your job to call the customer and deliver this bad news. You decide, since this customer is usually very assertive, to be direct and to the point. You know the customer will demand the original date be kept. So you must be prepared to be firm. You also know this customer will not be very interested in why the date is not going to be met.

CSR: "I wanted to let you know that the date I gave you, the 16th, is incorrect. Your delivery date will be the 20th. I hope this doesn't cause too much of an inconvenience."

CUSTOMER: "It does! I need the 16th."

CSR: "I understand, but we can't meet the 16th. The 20th is a firm date that I can guarantee."

CUSTOMER: "Who do I talk with to get the 16th?"

CSR: "I wish there was someone. My manager has been involved and we looked into every possibility, but the best we can offer is the 20th. As you know, we seldom miss a quoted delivery date, but unfortunately this is one of those rare situations."

CUSTOMER: "This is unsatisfactory service."

CSR: "I understand your feelings. Again, my apologies. In the future I will personally verify your dates before quoting them. That way, mistakes like this will be avoided."

CUSTOMER: "They should have been verified this time."

CSR: "You are absolutely correct, and I can assure you they will be in the future."

Let's analyze this conversation. If you were listening in on this exchange, you would have heard a concise, businesslike conversation in which the customer expressed her dissatisfaction. Despite her brief responses, she did not raise her voice. The customer is being assertive, not angry. Even though the CSR responded to the assertive customer in an appropriate manner, the customer is still not satisfied and wants the 16th date. But, the customer received an apology and some assurance that the difficulty won't occur again. If the CSR is able to deliver on that promise, the customer will be satisfied in the long run. What would you have done differently? Would you have taken a softer approach, such as explaining why the date was misquoted?

Every CSR facing a difficult situation will approach it a little differently. In our example the assertive customer is very direct, focused on the business side, and wants results. The CSR responds accordingly. Notice that he did not go into an explanation of why the date was incorrect. Nor did the customer ask for one—this is typical assertive customer behavior. Assertive customers are generally not interested in the "why" of a situation. The CSR did a wise thing in taking the extra step to provide some assurance that this problem will not happen in the future.

THE DETAIL-FOCUSED CUSTOMER

We've seen how the assertive customer usually has little interest in the "why" and "how" of a situation or problem. In contrast, a detail-focused customer requires this type of information. This individual is motivated by accuracy and appreciates detail. This type of customer wants a lot of information before they make a decision. They want to take time to analyze and think about their decision.

If you are assertive by nature and want fast action, this type of customer will be a challenge for you. You may have to slow down, provide plenty of supportive information, and then show patience while the customer decides. This customer will want the details of nearly every situation. If there is a new customer policy, for instance, they will want the basis for it, because it's important for their understanding.

The detail-focused customer shares one trait with the assertive personality: little interest in the relationship side of business. They may even seem cold as they pursue accuracy and supporting information. Social conversation may be difficult for detail-focused individuals, unless you are talking about subjects of interest to them. They will generally not add a comment just to be polite; small talk isn't their forte.

A CONVERSATION WITH A DETAIL-FOCUSED CUSTOMER

Let's rearrange the earlier example of the delivery date that had to be changed to the 20th. Speaking with a detail-focused customer, the conversation might have gone like this:

CSR:	"I wanted to let you know that the delivery date I gave you was incorrect. We can't deliver on the 16th, but we can meet the 20th. I know this is not what you wanted, but the demand for our products has increased so much that we have, for the first time, been unable to meet all the dates promised. The good news is, we have taken steps to correct this situation. I can guarantee the quoted dates will be good in the future. I hope this doesn't cause too much of a problem for you."
CUSTOMER:	"Well, let's see, my engineering people won't like this delay. I don't understand—I gave you plenty of time. What is this, some sort of a backlog problem?"
CSR:	"Basically, you're right—but it's only temporary. On your next order I can guarantee the delivery date."
CUSTOMER:	"So you have cleared your backlog?"
CSR:	"We expect it to be gone within the next few days."

CUSTOMER: "So have you increased production?"

CSR: "Yes, we had to do that because of the high demand for our product. We also have a new order-entry system going in that will provide even faster service. Again, I'm sorry for this inconvenience."

Notice how this situation was managed differently for each customer. In the assertive customer situation, none of the backlog and new order-entry information was shared, but he does share it with the detail-focused customer who is searching for facts, reasons, and accuracy. The customer still may not be satisfied with the date change, but he is probably satisfied about the reasons for the change. At a minimum, he gets supportive information. When this customer informs his engineering group of the missed delivery date, he will use the reasons given for the delay as part of his explanation. (In contrast, the assertive customer would simply relay that the date had slipped. The engineers, who are usually focused on details, might insist on more information from the assertive individual. In this situation it's easy to see where conflict can arise.)

One more thought on this situation: Note how the CSR stated the reasons for the missed date in positive terms, by talking about "high product demand" and "new order-entry system." It's important to keep customer input as positive as possible and avoid sharing negative information.

THE RELATIONSHIP-BASED CUSTOMER

The third customer behavior style we will consider is the friendly/relating type. These customers base much of their business activity on relationships with other people, including the CSRs they do business with. They see nearly everyone as someone to "work with," and they like the idea of working jointly to resolve problems and reduce conflict.

Typically, relationship-based people are put off by aggressive or assertive behavior. They avoid conflict and confrontation at nearly any cost. Strong team players, they are easy to get along with and work with. In most customer service situations, the relator will spend some time on the relationship side before getting down to business. If you have a problem providing the needed service, these customers will be more understanding than your assertive customers might be. They are motivated by working together without conflict.

RISKS ASSOCIATED WITH THE RELATIONSHIP-BASED CUSTOMER

On the surface, it would appear that customers who want to build relationships are the easiest to satisfy—and that's often true. But don't make the mistake of taking this customer for granted. It's common for CSRs to assume this customer is satisfied because of a lack of complaints. This customer avoids conflict and is unlikely to demand better service or register complaints. While the typical assertive customer is complaining loudly over a service problem, the relationship-based customer is trying to find a solution—and if that fails may simply withdraw from the conflict. Unfortunately, that withdrawal may include finding someone new to do business with. This customer won't announce that they're leaving; they simply won't be your customer anymore.

In situations where there is a lack of a satisfying relationship, or when confronted with a CSR who is too assertive, the relationship-based customer may easily experience dissatisfaction and even hurt feelings. Again, you won't hear much of a complaint. But watch out; the quieter they are, the more dissatisfied they may be.

The key to success with relationship-oriented customers is, of course, establishing and maintaining a productive relationship. This relationship should be warm, friendly, and may include sharing personal information. For best results, emphasize cooperation and working together.

WHAT'S YOUR STYLE?

Did you get a sense of your own behavioral style as you read the preceding sections? Are you primarily assertive, detailed-oriented, or relationship-based? In terms of working with customers, having one particular style doesn't give you any special advantage. What you need is versatility—the ability to modify your behavioral style in order to work successfully with others. People are generally a combination of the three styles, with one style being dominant. The assertive personality, for instance, may also be able to work with details and can function in a team environment when necessary. It's definitely not the assertive person's preferred method of working, but if their versatility is strong enough, they can do it. Versatility is the key for most CSRs.

The two steps to improving your versatility are

1. Understand your own style.

2. Recognize and appropriately respond to the customer's style.

How do you rate your versatility? Are you flexible enough to satisfy customers who are different from you? Use the following scale to rate your level of versatility to satisfy the different customer styles. A rating of 1 is poor; if you feel your versatility is high, give yourself a 5.

	Circle One				
Assertive Customers	1	2	3	4	5
Detailed-Oriented Customers	1	2	3	4	5
Relationship-Oriented Customers	1	2	3	4	5

Most CSRs find that they respond with a different level of versatility depending on the type of customer they encounter. The rating scale you've just completed will help you focus on any area that needs improvement. With this information in mind, here's a short summary of tips that will help you recognize and work with the customer behaviors you encounter in your CSR work.

MATCHING YOUR STYLE TO THAT OF YOUR CUSTOMER

The assertive customer wants results and fast action. If you're relationship oriented, don't expect much social interaction and don't be offended by the customer's abruptness. If you like to work with details, it's important to remember the assertive customer is generally concerned with the bottom line. Don't try to provide a lot of details because the assertive customer isn't interested. If you tend to speak slowly, pick up the pace, focus on what's important, and don't assume the customer is angry.

The detail-oriented customer seeks accuracy and to be correct. The facts, the figures and the details are important to this person in making the right decision. If you can't provide what they want, you must provide the reasons. Don't expect very much on the relationship side from this customer, because he is not focused in that direction. If your style is assertive and you are speaking with a detail-oriented customer, it's important to slow down and focus on supporting information rather than just the end result.

The relationship-oriented customer wants to know you and to work together to solve problems. If you are a detail-oriented or assertive person and are trying to satisfy this type of customer, a relationship must be established. Working with people who are very direct and assertive may offend this type of customer.

MANAGING THE CUSTOMER'S PERCEPTION

Every customer has a mental image of the organizations with which they do business. You may have served some of your most important customers, strictly on the telephone, over a long period of time without having ever met them face to face. Even so, the CSR and customer both can easily describe each other. They have simply acquired a mental perception of each other and of their respective organizations. In fact, it's impossible for a customer *not* to form a perception of these organizations. This perception begins with the first contact and continues for the life of the business relationship.

Customer perceptions are affected by a plethora of factors, such as

- The CSR's ability to meet commitments
- Tact and honesty in response to customer inquiries or when handling negative service situations
- Ability to follow-up on service problems
- Common courtesy
- Follow-up after new or large orders
- Everyday conversations
- The CSR's attitude in general
- Advance notice of scheduled price increases
- The efficiency of the CSR
- The CSR's willingness to help

Almost everything said and done by the CSR and the organization affects the customer's perception. Perhaps a routine telephone call begins forming the perception. The telephone is answered promptly with a courteous tone, the CSR is knowledgeable, and as a result the customer is satisfied with the service received. Even though the call may have lasted only a few minutes, the customer acquires a positive perception of the CSR and the organization.

It's unavoidable that problems will occur, and it's your job to manage the customer's perception under these circumstances, as well. Since we want the customer to have a positive perception, it's important to take steps to ensure that this happens. It's part of your responsibility as a CSR to manage the customer's perception.

THE KEY TO MANAGING CUSTOMER PERCEPTION

The CSR is often the customer's primary point of contact and as a result has the most influence on the customer's perception. The key for the

CSR in managing this perception is to *produce a customer-satisfying experience with each contact.*

Sounds simple, doesn't it? However, as experienced CSRs have learned, creating a customer-satisfying experience with each telephone call or meeting is difficult to say the least. Certain factors must be in place. In Section I, we discussed three factors:

- The structure of service

- Management policies

- Actions of frontline personnel

The CSR can influence the first two and has considerable control over the third. The degree to which these factors are delivered and managed by the CSR has great impact on the customer's satisfaction and perception.

To satisfy a customer, you must first understand what the customer wants. Next, you must have the skills to provide as many of those wants and needs as possible. Within your customer service group, you might develop a list of typical customer needs. For example:

- Fast response

- Timely service

- Fair pricing

- Courtesy

- Promises kept

- Knowledgeable CSR

- Advice and counsel when appropriate

- Accuracy

- Consistent service

There are a host of other customer needs and wants—it's common to have 20 or 30. The goal for you and your CSR team is to satisfy as many of these wants as possible.

EXAMPLES OF MANAGING CUSTOMER PERCEPTION

Positive customer perceptions are created when the customer's expectations are met. The customer expects a particular level of service, the CSR delivers, and a positive perception is created. In our earlier example of shopping at a 30% Off sale, the customer's expectation for service was low, but it was high for saving money. The store created an environment during this sale where the customer's expectations were met. The CSR, in a sense, does the same thing.

EVERYTHING YOU SAY IS IMPORTANT

Your customer's perception is influenced by nearly everything you say and do. Some statements and responses help create the desired perceptions; others will detract from it. Take a look at the following 10 statements. After reading each statement, ask yourself what impact these statements would have on the customer's perception of the CSR and the organization. Will the statement be perceived as positive or negative? Judge for yourself.

		Positive	*Negative*
1.	I can't help you with that. You'll have to call Software Support.	❑	❑
2.	Wow! This is really a mess. I don't know how they got your billing so confused. Have you been paying everything on time?	❑	❑
3.	Sure, I'll be glad to help you.	❑	❑
4.	I'm sorry, can you repeat the problem to me? I didn't get it all the first time.	❑	❑

5. Please call me any time. It was a pleasure   ❑   ❑
    talking to you.

6. May I review your order to make certain   ❑   ❑
    it's accurate?

7. We appreciate your business.   ❑   ❑

8. Good morning, this is Bryan Apple.   ❑   ❑
    How may I help you?

9. Acme Wholesale Electronics, please hold.   ❑   ❑

10. Let me check that for you. Do you mind   ❑   ❑
    holding for a moment?

Each of these statements will have an impact on the customer. Certainly the larger issues such as product satisfaction and the structure of service are extremely important, but the everyday actions of the CSR also play a vital role in shaping customer perception. Every statement or action is mentally recorded by the customer as either positive or negative. This subconscious recording helps build the customer's perception of the CSR and the organization in general.

IV

WORKSHOP: DEVELOPING CUSTOMER SATISFACTION SKILLS

So far we have discussed the important topics of professionalism and customer knowledge and the vital role they play in bringing about customer satisfaction. Your professionalism and customer knowledge are demonstrated through your CSR skills. The greater these skills, the more your customers are satisfied. In this section, we'll move into a practical workshop in the key skills that a CSR needs to be successful. Most basic CSR skills are well documented in other publications, so we'll address only a few of these. You'll want to refer to *Telephone Courtesy and Customer Service,* by this author, for a detailed presentation. For all CSRs, a periodic review of the basic skills of customer communication is helpful and recommended.

THE SKILLS

The 11 skills described in this section are part of every successful CSR's tool kit. It's what you bring to your job and use throughout the day.

- **Skill 1:** The Steps of a Customer Conversation

- **Skill 2:** Listening to the Customer

- **Skill 3:** Basic Communication

- **Skill 4:** Determining Customer Satisfaction
- **Skill 5:** Fact-Finding
- **Skill 6:** Asking Questions
- **Skill 7:** Product Knowledge
- **Skill 8:** Working Toward a Stronger Relationship
- **Skill 9:** Developing and Implementing an Action Plan
- **Skill 10:** Smaller Action Plans
- **Skill 11:** Self-Appraisal

You have a variety of customers, and therefore the skills in your tool kit vary, as well. Fact finding may be the key in one customer conversation; in another, employing the five important steps of every customer conversation may make a positive difference.

The skills presented here are designed to improve your customer communication abilities. The experienced, successful CSR can use these experiences to enhance an already strong performance. If you are new to customer service or want to upgrade your skill level, you can use these skills as a stepping stone to greater success. These skills can be put into practice immediately. Follow the suggestions and watch your performance improve even more.

SKILL 1: THE STEPS OF A CUSTOMER CONVERSATION

There are five steps to every customer conversation. In most situations, all five steps apply to both incoming and outgoing customer calls, and face-to-face meetings. We will study additional information about these basic steps throughout Section IV.

STEP 1: GREET THE CUSTOMER

- Identify yourself, and your department or work unit.
- Say "Good morning" or "Good afternoon," or something like "It's nice to hear from you again."
- Make the customer feel welcome.
- Convey that you are glad to be talking with the customer.
- Use an enthusiastic tone of voice.
- Give your full attention to the call or meeting.
- Be friendly.

STEP 2: ESTABLISH RAPPORT

What does it mean to have rapport with a customer? Creating rapport does not mean you and the customer engage in a lot of social conversation. Rather, you build rapport by demonstrating competence, and by assisting or advising the customer. Rapport is more of a feeling than anything else. You and the customer know you can work well together. You may have developed a style that has often been called a "shirt-sleeve environment," in which you and the customer sit side by side and resolve issues and problems of the customer. It doesn't mean you are great friends or exchange much in the way of social conversation. Although it's important that you are friendly, warm, and welcoming toward the customer, the rapport will usually be based on your competence.

Earlier we discussed the customer's behavior style. When you are trying to establish rapport, the customer's behavior/personality style is important. Use the following guidelines:

- When the customer's personality is relationship-based, spend some time developing the relationship.

- When the customer is assertive or detail-oriented, it's still important to spend a little time on the relationship side. Try a simple "How is everything?" The customer's response will tell you if they are interested in more social conversation.

- Recall and use information from a previous call with the customer (if appropriate). For example, "Last time we talked, you said you were reading the material I sent. How did that work out for you?" Other examples: "I have your billing and shipping address from the last order." or "Have you had time to think about our discussion regarding your new office and the system you will need?"

STEP 3: CLARIFY THE PURPOSE OF THE CALL OR MEETING

- Create a friendly environment that makes the customer feel comfortable.

- Stay focused on the purpose of the call and work toward satisfying that purpose. Avoid being distracted.

- If the customer's purpose in calling is unclear, ask questions about it.

STEP 4: FACT-FINDING

- When appropriate, conduct fact-finding to learn about the customer. (See Skills 5 and 6.)

- By understanding the customer's operation, and their product or service application, you can better serve the customer.

- Determine the following:

  1. Is there an opportunity to advise and counsel the customer?

  2. Are there complementary products or services the customer may need?

  3. Does the customer need further assistance?

4. What are the customer's future plans?

5. When should you follow up?

STEP 5: PRESENT THE ACTION PLAN

- When appropriate, discuss the next step with the customer. For instance, "I'll take care of this order immediately, and your delivery date will be the 17th." "I'll research your question and get back to you by three o'clock."

- Keep the customer's behavior style in mind. Assertive customers want a short, to-the-point action plan. Detail-oriented customers usually want the "how" and "why" of the action plan.

- After stating the action plan, close the conversation with an appropriate sign-off. "Thanks for calling." "We appreciate your business."

- Follow through as promised.

These five basic steps usually flow together and, in practice, are much less formal than they may appear. All customers want to work in a comfortable environment, and you can create that with every call or meeting by following these five steps.

SKILL 2: LISTENING TO THE CUSTOMER

The CSR who knows how to listen possesses an invaluable skill. It is simply a must. The CSR needs to listen to

- What the customer says and how it is said
- Where the customer is placing emphasis in order to respond appropriately
- What the customer is requesting
- Signs of customer satisfaction

CONFIRM WHAT YOU HEAR

Part of listening is the confirmation process. For example, say you've taken a complex order. Getting confirmation is stating, "Let me quickly review your order." In other instances, you might need to review the action plan and confirm it. When the customer is detail oriented, confirmation provides considerable assurance. Key details don't get missed. When the customer is assertive, you should discuss only the most important details, and even they may be reduced if the customer shows a lack of interest.

ACTORS AS TEACHERS OF LISTENING SKILLS

To gain insight into the listening process, watch actors "listen." Most dialogue on television or in the movies is between two people. One talks and the other listens. Good actors know how to listen. They show rapt attention, often confirming that they are listening through facial expressions or gestures like a nod or some sort of body or hand movement. When the actor is skilled, you can read his or her reaction to what is heard even though the actor may not utter a word.

When meeting face to face with customers, many of these same techniques and skills will work for you. Maintain eye contact, not with an intense state but with an "I am interested" look. On the telephone, of course, you won't have access to body language or eye contact, so use verbal communications to tell the customer you're listening. Use short confirming comments like "I see," "Yes," "I understand," and "Of course." At other times, complete silence is required, but don't allow too much time to pass without a confirmation that you're listening. If your customer has to ask, "Are you there?" it's bad news. The occasional confirming comment is a must.

SKILL 3: BASIC COMMUNICATION

This section is about the common skills a CSR must practice in customer conversations. When CSRs learn what these skills are, they usually respond with "Oh, those—I already know them." Of course, you may already know of these basic skills, but to what extent do you practice them? Hopefully, your answer is, "with every customer conversation." These are fundamental communication skills that are effective and customer satisfying. Let's start with courtesy.

EXTENDING COURTESY

Just as customers want to feel welcome and comfortable, they also want to be treated courteously. This should be automatic behavior for the CSR. Courtesy is more than remembering to say "thank you" and "you're welcome." It's an attitude that the customer hears and feels.

The customer who places considerable business with your organization wants to hear the CSR say thank you, but it's even more important that your actions do the same. When an order needs expediting or an invoice needs explaining, or any other request needs handling, the CSR extends courtesy by simply taking care of the request. "I'll be glad to handle that for you."

Treat the customer in a courteous manner regardless of the situation. Suppose the customer is angry, hostile, or aggressive. You listen to the reasons for the anger, avoid getting caught up in the emotion of the moment, speak courteously to the customer, and hopefully find an acceptable solution. Professionalism requires that the CSR remain courteous despite the customer's attitude.

SAYING THANK-YOU

At the conclusion of the conversation, you can simply say one of the following thank-you's:

- Thanks for calling.
- Thanks for your order.
- We appreciate your business.

- Please feel free to call any time. I enjoyed talking with you.
- Thanks for your business.
- Please call again.
- Your call is always welcome.
- I look forward to talking with you in the future.

How you close the conversation is important because it strongly influences the customer's perception of the organization and the CSR. Suppose a customer places several orders. Even if you present yourself as knowledgeable and courteous, and overall the conversation goes well, forgetting to say "thanks for your call" or "thanks for your order" means a failure to show appreciation. The customer may simply overlook your error, but he or she may feel slighted. Maybe the customer says to herself, "If they don't appreciate my business, I can order those ugly widgets somewhere else." Most customers, in fact, will react to this "lack of appreciation"—and that response will typically be negative.

MORE ABOUT CLOSING THE CONVERSATION

Closing the conversation correctly also requires timing. Ideally, the conversation is closed when the customer is through talking, but that doesn't always work. Some customers talk a lot and, with other customers waiting, you must skillfully manage the closing of the conversation. This means moving the conversation toward a close without rushing the customer. You can't, for example, just say "thanks for your business" and hang up. Here are some expressions to help you.

- *"I think that covers everything. Do you have any questions?"*

  (The customer says No, you thank the customer, and end the conversation.)

- *"As I said, everything will ship on Friday. I want you to know we appreciate your business."*

  (The customer thanks you, and you can then say "I enjoyed talking with you.")

- *"Let me quickly review your order."*

  (Then do this quickly and say, "We appreciate your business and thanks for calling.")

- *"I know you're busy, so I won't keep you. Thanks for calling."*

BE CONVERSATIONAL

Another basic but critical CSR skill is the ability to be conversational with the customer. Too often the CSR is tied to completing an order form or a screen format. In the quest for needed information from the customer, you may without thinking blurt out question after question, in rapid-fire order. It may sound something like this:

CUSTOMER:	I want to order two blue widgets.
CSR:	The name of your company?
CUSTOMER:	Alpha Omega Industries.
CSR:	Your address?
CUSTOMER:	2376 Mariposa Street, Baltimore
CSR:	The Zip Code?

. . . And the conversation continues this way until the CSR has filled in all the lines, dotted the i's and crossed the t's. The CSR focuses more on the order format than on the customer. Let's see how this exchange could be more conversational.

CUSTOMER:	I want to order two blue widgets.

At this point the CSR might compliment the customer on her selection or make some other acknowledging comment—maybe one of the following:

YOU: That's a good choice.

I think you'll like the blue widgets.

This has been one of our best sellers.

If you get a response, acknowledge it.

Next, you should advise the customer that she will be asked a few questions.

YOU: I'll need to ask you a few questions for the order.

Let me ask a few questions in order to complete your order.

From this point, each question you ask is spoken courteously.

YOU: May I have the name of your organization and your address?

Are the Ship To and the Bill To address the same?

Will you be using a purchase order number?

May I address the shipment to your attention?

May I have your phone number please?

How these routine questions are asked is important. The statements as phrased here are more pleasing to the customer's ear and certainly more professional. Remember, the customer's perception of the organization—and you—is created by everything the customer hears from you. Common courtesy is a must!

DISCUSSING THE COMPETITION

In the course of discussing products and services with the customer, names of competing companies or products will likely come up. Be careful what you say about competitors. When it's appropriate, you can offer a comparison of your products with the competitor's. Often there is no requirement to offer any comparison; instead, you can simply acknowledge the competitor. The customer, for example, says, "I've been using XYZ product." At this point, you can simply ask, "How is the XYZ product working for you?" Next, you need to get back to discussing your own product. Above all else, avoid making disparaging remarks about the competitor. It is far better to discuss and point out the advantages of your product and service than it is to run down the competition.

NOTE: Some CSRs feel they have to praise the competitor. At times this may be appropriate, but it should always be kept to a minimum.

COMMUNICATION TIP

In the midst of trying to satisfy customers, the basics are often overlooked. Courtesy is always a must. Make certain that the customer is greeted and made to feel welcome. When a customer places an order, show appreciation. Customers should always hear "thanks for calling." Every CSR can put the basics into practice.

SKILL 4: DETERMINING CUSTOMER SATISFACTION

Many organizations conduct formal customer surveys for the purpose of determining satisfaction levels. On an ongoing basis, the CSR as well must find out whether their individual customers are satisfied. In determining customer satisfaction, there is a basic rule to follow: DON'T ASSUME! It is foolish to make assumptions about customer satisfaction.

By asking, you gain valuable insight and avoid being deceived. When the customer *expresses* satisfaction, you *know* the service provided is satisfactory.

WHEN TO ASK

Obviously, you can't ask the customer each time you have a conversation if they are satisfied with the service received. However, there are appropriate situations and instances when the customer should be asked. Here are a few:

- Following a protracted or complex customer situation
- When a long-term customer may have been taken for granted
- When the irate customer has eventually received what has been requested
- When the customer is new
- When the customer's account is large
- When there is the slightest doubt that you have satisfied the customer

Here are a few examples of how to ask the customer about their level of satisfaction:

- I'm sorry this took so long to resolve. Is it resolved to your satisfaction?
- We talk quite often, but I never seem to get a chance to ask if you are satisfied with our service. How do you feel about our service?
- I know you were upset when we started working on this. How do you feel about our service now?

- We appreciate your business. If you don't mind, may I ask how you rate our service?

- As you know your account is very important to us and we want you to be satisfied. How do you rate the service we're providing?

An important question to ask customers periodically is, "How can we (or I) improve the service you receive?"

Most CSRs don't take the time to ask their customers these important questions. Be the exception and eliminate any doubt—ask. The service you provide will be even more valuable if you understand the customer's thoughts and opinions about your service.

USING A CUSTOMER PROFILE

Customer profiles are a common tool for understanding the customer's key concerns and issues. Obviously, knowledge of the customer's needs means stronger customer service—especially when the CSR works over time with the same customer. In this situation, the customer profile can be used to develop considerable information regarding the customer and the account. An important part of this profile is determining the level of customer satisfaction for every service received. With a small account, knowing their level of satisfaction may be enough. However, with a larger account or a critical customer, that is just the beginning.

To reduce the risk of the key account becoming dissatisfied, the CSR should know the customer's level of satisfaction on all issues. A service profile can be developed that, at a glance, provides a summary of the customer's position on the key issues affecting service. The profile can also be the basis for discussion with the customer and for developing an action plan for service improvement. An example of such a profile in shown on page 76.

CUSTOMER PROFILE

Account Name: *Wilson Widgets Inc.*

		SATISFACTION LEVEL		
Customer issue or concern: _____ _____	***Unsatisfied***	***Somewhat Satisfied***	***Satisfied***	***Completely Satisfied***
CSR communications			*	
Response Time		*		
Accuracy of information			*	
CSR product knowledge				*
CSR resolution of problems		*		
Dates met		*		
Price of products/services				*
System performance				*
Structure of service				*
Management policies				*
CSR trustworthiness			*	
Reliability of service			*	
Trend of service (positive or negative?				

Of course, the issues identified on the profile depend upon the account and the customer. When it's a large account, and the CSR interfaces with several customers, each of these customers will have separate issues and concerns and may require an individual profile. For example, separate profiles might be maintained for a key decision maker, an office manager, and a purchasing manager.

With this type of information, how much easier do you think it will be to provide quality service? Further, suppose a new CSR is assigned to the account. Do you think the transition between CSRs will be smoother? It stands to reason that, with the customer information available, the new CSR can step right in and take over.

Remember, much of customer satisfaction is created because you understand the customer and provide the level of service they want. The greater knowledge you have, the easier it will be to satisfy the customer.

SHARING THE PROFILE WITH THE CUSTOMER

With particular accounts or customers, it may be appropriate to use the profile as a service "review" as a means of building a stronger relationship. With the review in hand, the next step is to meet with the customer to define and discuss the key issues. This approach gives the CSR an excellent opportunity to move closer to the customer and strengthen the working relationship. The customer has a platform to give valuable input on the service received. Customer concerns and problems can be discussed, and action plans developed to resolve these issues. Sound like a lot of work? It is, but why take risks with large accounts? Develop the profile with your customer's input, and you have an invaluable tool for service improvement.

SKILL 5: FACT-FINDING

Developing a customer or large account profile requires *fact-finding* skills. Fact-finding ability is an absolute requirement for the CSR, especially in high-end jobs where multiple products or services are offered. CSR advancement and opportunity may well depend upon the CSR's ability to conduct fact-finding and obtain valuable customer information.

Successful fact-finding has many benefits. For example, fact-finding helps determine and resolve customer problems and can create opportunities for cross-selling. New or different product applications can be uncovered; future plans can be learned. Fact-finding is yet another means of adding to your knowledge and understanding of your customers, which helps build a stronger relationship and increases the probability of larger orders and future business.

A common way to begin learning fact-finding skills is to ask, "What is it I would like to know about the customer?" Suppose a customer calls and orders 10 widgets. As the CSR you gather all the order information. Then you might thank the caller for the order and close the conversation. This is exactly what most CSRs do. But suppose you want to know if there are additional opportunities for selling your products or services. What questions about the customer would you like to have answered?

Here's a list of 10 questions that apply to the customer's widget order.

TEN FACT-FINDING QUESTIONS

1. What is the application for our widgets?
2. Who made the decision to order the widgets?
3. Does your firm have other locations where widgets can be used?
4. Are you currently using other widgets?
5. If you're using our competitor's widgets, are you satisfied with them?

6. Why did you decide to order our widgets over the competitor's?

7. How did you hear about our widgets?

8. Are you familiar with our large and superlarge widget product lines?

9. Do you have one of our new brochures/catalogs?

10. What are your future plans for using these and other widgets?

The 10 questions shown above are fairly standard. In your particular job and organization, additional questions may apply.

The answers to these questions will be helpful in many ways. Obviously, they create opportunities for expanded business. They also help you anticipate future needs, and possibly identify additional product applications. The customer will also benefit because you will provide a higher level of service through your improved knowledge of the product application and the customer's operation. Armed with this knowledge, you can provide advice, counseling, and appropriate recommendations.

HOW TO ASK FACT-FINDING QUESTIONS

Fact finding is not necessarily easy; but it can be learned and, with practice and effort, successfully used. Don't be concerned with the order of the questions, because they will typically be asked as opportunities occur within the initial order conversation. For example, the customer might mention one of your competitors immediately. Or perhaps the caller wants a new price list. Be prepared to fit an appropriate question into the conversation at the right time.

Let's figure out *how* to ask these questions.

You might say, "I have ten questions to ask. Do you have a few moments?" This is an unprofessional approach that would rarely work. The task is to skillfully ask these questions *as part of the normal customer conversation,* and to be conversational about it.

CAUTION: If you handle customer orders, be certain that the order doesn't get unhooked in the process of fact finding. In other words, don't create confusion or indecision in the customer's mind to the point where the original order gets delayed or canceled. This can happen, for instance, if the fact-finding reveals the customer should have ordered a different product or service; in this case, the change is okay. But if the discussion gets so involved that the customer becomes confused and unsure enough to cancel or postpone the order, that's unacceptable. As a general rule, try to secure the order first unless the customer is ordering incorrectly or absolutely needs to review the purchase decision. The risk of delaying or losing an order is one more reason the fact-finding needs to be skillfully conducted.

How do you manage this "conversational" fact-finding? Step one, as discussed, is to take the customer's order and gather the necessary order information. Step two is to start probing for more information and potential opportunities for added products or services. Here's an example of how this might roll out. We'll use our widget order example again.

CSR: How did you hear about our widgets?

CUSTOMER: Last year I looked at one of your catalogs. I thought we might need a few widgets at some point so I kept it in our files.

CSR: We have a new catalog. I'll send one to you.

CUSTOMER: Thanks. That's a good idea.

CSR: Who else in your organization should I send one to?

CUSTOMER: Mine will be enough.

CSR: If you don't mind my asking, will all future orders come from you?

CUSTOMER: Yes. I do most of the buying for our division.

CSR: We like to build account information in order to provide better service. Shall I put your name in as the decision maker?

CUSTOMER: My boss actually makes the final decisions, but I always collect all the information for her.

CSR: I know that you will be our contact, but may I have her name for our account information records?

CUSTOMER: Sure. It's Sandy Rogers. She's the Admin Manager.

CSR: Thanks. Do you have responsibility for other company locations as well?

CUSTOMER: We only have one other location, our Wilmington factory.

CSR: Would you order for them as well?

CUSTOMER: Yes, I'd handle that.

CSR: Are they using widgets as part of the operation?

CUSTOMER: I think they have about 100 installed.

CSR: That's quite a few. I don't show a Wilmington location as one of our widget installation locations. You must be using CoreRam or the Miser models.

CUSTOMER: Most of them are CoreRam.

CSR: CoreRam sure created much of this industry with their 811s. How well are they working for you?

CUSTOMER: They have been very reliable, but your new features are of interest to us. We think we can cut some of our delay time with your widgets.

CSR: Some of our customers report delay time reduction of 20%. I think you will find similar reductions.

CUSTOMER: I hope so.

CSR: When you get our catalog, take a look at our large and superlarge widgets. They may fit well with your plans for the Wilmington factory. By the way, do you plan to change out those CoreRam widgets?

CUSTOMER: No. It's too early to talk about that.

CSR: I understand. Do you have any questions?

CUSTOMER: No, I think we're all set.

CSR: Thanks for your order, Ted. We appreciate your business.

SERVICE OR SALES?

In this case, the CSR was successful, and a short conversation revealed quite a bit of information. The CSR simply asked Ted questions that fit well within the conversation. Ted was willing to talk, and that added to the success of the fact-finding.

Some CSRs, upon reading our sample conversation, might say, "Those were not service skills that were demonstrated; they were sales skills." Actually, it is a *higher level* of service skills. The CSR makes no attempt to upgrade or to cross-sell the customer into a different product, but rather is just seeking customer information that may lead to increased orders or future business. This was done in a professional manner. Depending upon the CSR's job, she might follow up with the customer or perhaps would refer the account to Sales for follow up.

As the CSR conducted the fact-finding, a sales opportunity might have developed. Suppose, for example, the customer had expressed more interest in the superlarge widgets. In this situation the CSR would have explained the value and benefits of the larger widget and perhaps taken a new order. Even so, it would still be more service than sales. Discussing various options, opportunities, and products with customers is part of the CSR's job. CSRs who do this well are a valuable resource.

A NOTE TO CUSTOMER-SERVICE MANAGERS:

Sales and service positions, of course, have different responsibilities and priorities. CSRs are involved with service because they enjoy providing service for customers. If they liked to sell, they would be in sales. This is an important distinction, especially for managers who want more of a sales effort from their CSRs. To expect CSRs to do fact-finding and learn more about the customer is one thing, but asking CSRs to consistently try to upgrade and cross-sell may not be reasonable. Besides, customers do not want to be faced with a sales attempt every time they call the customer service center.

SUPPOSE THE CUSTOMER DOESN'T WANT TO TALK

Not every customer will want to share information with you or have the time to do so. In a sales situation, the salesperson is expected to try to continue the conversation and will make several attempts to do so. In a service environment, however, you need to observe the customer's responses with care. If the customer doesn't want to talk or answer questions, thank the customer and then end the conversation. This is especially true in an order situation. When the customer places an order and then indicates he doesn't want more conversation, you must allow the conversation to end. In this way, the order remains secure—and that's the first priority of the CSR.

ANALYZING OUR FACT-FINDING QUESTIONS

Let's look at the questions we asked, studying when and how they were asked. The CSR began with

"How did you hear about our widgets?"

This is a logical question to ask and one the customer is familiar with. It usually opens the door for further questions or added discussion. The customer's reply was "Last year I looked at your catalog." Since it was last year's catalog, the CSR offers to send a new one.

The logical follow up to the catalog offer was the question

"Who else in your organization should I send one to?"

Think about the possibilities the customer's answer might bring. You can easily learn about other locations and potential buyers. The follow-up might be to simply send catalogs, brochures, or price lists to the people and places mentioned, or even do an introductory telephone call. If the potential is substantial, the sales unit might be alerted. A lot of valuable information can be gained from asking a basic question.

The customer says there isn't anyone else in his organization who needs a catalog. The CSR then asks a critical question:

"Will all future orders come from you?"

The answer is Yes, and this identifies the caller as the primary source for future orders. However, we still don't know who the decision maker is. This information may not always be important. However, when it's a large account or sizable order, knowing and working with the decision maker is crucial. It certainly was for Kelly in the illustration below.

Where Did the Account Go?

Kelly became concerned when she had not heard from one of her key customers, Quality Systems, in quite a while. Her primary contact was Purchasing Agent John Miller. John would call almost every week to place orders, check the status of orders, or make inquiries, and his working relationship with Kelly was excellent.

On more than one occasion John had told her, "I really should place the order with your competition because on several items their prices are a little cheaper and the products are the same. But manufacturing prefers your products." John also preferred to place the orders with Kelly because of the outstanding service he had always received from her.

To determine why she hasn't heard from John, Kelly calls the Purchasing department at Quality Systems and learns that John no longer works there. She talks with his replacement, who tells her, "I've been ordering from your competitor because their pricing is a little better." Kelly responds, "But your manufacturing people prefer our products." The new purchasing agent says "I didn't know that. Who in manufacturing told you that?" Kelly doesn't have an answer.

Kelly's next course of action is difficult at best. She needs to find out who in Quality Systems's manufacturing unit is the decision maker, and who actually said they preferred her products. If she'd already obtained this name from John, she could simply make a quick call to that person. Knowing who the decision maker is would give her some recourse, rather than being faced with the uphill task she now faces.

Let's get back to the fact-finding conversation. The CSR decides to ask about the decision maker and says,

"We like to build account information in order to provide better service. Shall I show you as the decision maker?"

The customer said his boss is the decision maker, and clarifies his own role by stating, "I always collect all the information for her." Next, the CSR simply asks for the boss's name. The CSR now knows Ted's role and who the decision maker is.

Now, the CSR asks about the customer's scope of responsibility. In doing so, the CSR also learns about other account locations and that the customer will place any future orders for the organization's other locations. By asking if the other location is using widgets as part of their operation, he finds out there are about 100 installed. The CSR knows they aren't his widgets, so he asks which one of the competitor's widget models is installed. He learns most of the installed widgets are CoreRam 811s (the competitor's product) and then asks:

"How well are they working for you?"

The CSR learns Ted is interested in cutting widget delay time. It's important to note that the CSR does not offer any negative comment regarding the competitor or their product. The CSR comments about the benefits of his widgets in reducing delay time and suggests the customer look at the super-large widgets when he gets the brochures. He next asks if the customer is planning on replacing the competitor's widgets. The customer simply says, "It's too early to talk about that," and the CSR lets the conversation end.

WHAT DID THE CSR LEARN?

The CSR asked 11 questions, made a few comments, and conducted a short, businesslike conversation. In the process, the following was learned:

1. The customer ordered 10 widgets.

2. The customer collects information for his boss, Sandy Rogers, who makes the buying decisions.

3. All future orders will come from the customer.

4. There are two customer locations. The Wilmington location has 100 widgets installed, mostly CoreRams.

5. The customer is interested in reducing widget delay time and likes the features of the CSR's widgets.

6. The customer may be planning on changing out the CoreRams widgets, but says, "It's too early to talk about that now."

Of course, not every conversation will flow as smoothly as our example. What it does show is that by asking the right questions at the right time, the CSR can gain valuable customer information. In our example, the next step is for the CSR to send the catalog and then follow with a phone call asking if there are any questions regarding the material. This action might be completed by the CSR or, in many organizations, the sales unit would follow up. Sales might also want a face-to-face meeting with the caller and the decision maker, Sandy Rogers. If the CSR refers the account to Sales, the salesperson will be well satisfied with the information provided by the CSR's fact-finding.

PRACTICE, PRACTICE, AND THEN PRACTICE SOME MORE!

Fact-finding is an essential part of most CSR jobs. Customer information is crucial for follow-up and future orders.

To begin fact-finding with a customer or to improve what is currently being done, make a list of questions you would like to ask. Mentally review your past conversations with customers, and think when these questions might logically be asked.

Role-play with a coworker. If at first the questions don't flow smoothly, don't worry about it. Just keep trying. If you're not comfortable asking questions, be willing to stretch your comfort zone. Push yourself with each call. With continued effort, the questions will become more automatic and a normal part of almost every customer conversation.

With a new customer, you might begin (as the CSR did in our example) by asking, "How did you hear about our _____ (product, company, etc.)." Above all, keep the conversation moving by making comments, asking questions, and listening to the customer's responses. Maintain a conversational and nonthreatening tone. Explain to the customer why you're asking, if that's appropriate. Don't be hesitant to ask—the worst thing that can happen is that the customer will refuse to answer. For the most part, customers are polite and will understand that part of your job is to seek out added opportunities to be of service.

SKILL 6: ASKING QUESTIONS

Most of us are familiar with the terms *open* and *closed* when used to define questions. Open and closed questions fit into every customer conversation and can be used to help manage the exchange and gather information. Let's review some of the ground rules for closed and open questions.

Closed questions are designed to produce a short response, or a Yes or No answer. When overused, closed questions sound controlling, intimidating, and can make the questioning process seem like an interrogation. Closed questions begin with words such as is, *can, do, will,* and *shall.* In the fact-finding example used in Skill 5, the CSR used the following closed questions:

- "Will any future orders come from you?"

- "Shall I show your name as the decision maker?"

- "Do you have responsibility for other company locations?"

- "May I have her name for our account records?"

- "Are they using widgets as part of their operation?"

- "Are you using CoreRam or Miser models?"

- "Do you plan to change out those CoreRam widgets?"

Open questions are designed to produce a longer response; when phrased properly, open questions can't be answered with a Yes or No. Open questions should encourage more customer conversation; they begin with words such as *how, who, what, where, when,* and *why.* The CSR in the Skill 5 example used three important open questions:

- "How did you hear about our widgets?"

- "Who else in your organization should I send a catalog to?"

- "How well are they (widgets) working for you?"

This customer was willing to discuss his situation, and the CSR didn't have to ask more open questions to encourage the conversation.

KNOWING WHEN TO USE OPEN/CLOSED QUESTIONS

Closed questions can give you more control and encourage brevity in any customer conversation; open questions will produce a lengthier customer response. With very talkative customers, closed questions are appropriate to shorten the conversation. When the customer is less talkative, open questions can help develop a conversation.

As a CSR, you need to listen to yourself and hear the type and number of questions you're asking. Listen to the kind of responses you're getting from customers. When you're not getting all the information you need, the use of open questions may be the answer. If your conversations are running a little long, more closed questions may help.

PUT QUESTIONS INTO YOUR NORMAL CONVERSATION

You've seen how it works to ask questions and let the customer talk. Allow the questions to be part of the normal conversation. When appropriate, acknowledge the customer's comment with a question rather than a statement. For example, the CSR in our fact-finding example learned from the customer that there is only one other location in Wilmington.

Upon hearing the customer's response, a less-experienced CSR might respond with something like "I see," or otherwise acknowledge what the customer said. In our example, the CSR continues trying to learn about the caller's scope of responsibility: "Would you order for them as well?" It's often important to know what kind of authority the customer has. By simply asking the right questions at the right time, this information can usually be obtained. Our CSR did it by asking questions such as "Will any future orders come from you?" and "Shall I show you as the decision maker?"

COMBINING QUESTIONS WITH "SETUP" STATEMENTS

Sometimes it's important to place a short statement before the question. The purpose is to "soften" or explain the reason for the question. In the previous example, the CSR was trying to find out the name of the decision maker. Rather than bluntly asking the customer if he was the decision maker, he states, "We like to build account information in order to provide better service." Afterward, the question seems reasonable: "Shall I show as the decision maker?"

The caller tells us his boss makes the decisions but that he is the person we should talk with. So we soften the next question by adding assurance for the customer: "I know you will be our contact, but may I have her name (the boss) for our account records?" Softening a question is not always necessary. Some customers will tell the CSR nearly anything, while others are more secretive about their organization, its future plans, and the decision-making process. Use your own good judgment. If you feel a customer is getting sensitive regarding a particular question, it's best to set up further questions by using a softer approach. In other situations, you may feel comfortable simply explaining why you are asking the question. Here are examples of setup statements:

- If you don't mind my asking, . . . (now the question)

- I know you're the decision maker, but . . . (the question)

- By the way, . . . (now the question)

- If I may, I would to like to ask . . . (now the question)

- If you should decide to buy our products, . . . (now the question)

- I'm curious about, . . . (now the question)

- If I may ask, . . . (now the question) e.g., how much have you budgeted for widgets?

These and other setup statements will fit easily in front of most questions.

TIP: Keep two things in mind when asking "sensitive" questions. First, it's okay to ask. Second, if the customer doesn't want to answer a particular question, she won't. When asking for information you think might be sensitive, use a setup statement in front of the question to soften it.

CHASING THE RABBIT

The CSR in our Skill 5 example continued to ask questions about the caller's authority until all the needed information was obtained. This is called "chasing the rabbit down the hole." The same thing can be done to seek out more facts about most relevant customer issues.

 The first question to be asked in this rabbit-chasing process is the lead-in question. This question paves the way for additional questions and sets the tone for the conversation. Usually the lead-in question is an open question, and sometimes it's one you already know the answer to. The idea is to get the conversation rolling. Here are some examples of lead-in questions:

- How do you plan to use the (your products or service)?
- How many (your products or service, or your competitor's) are you currently using?
- How well are they working for you?
- Have you considered trying (your new, larger, or different product)?
- How did you hear about us?
- Do you have one of our price lists?
- Are you familiar with our discount pricing program?
- Have you used our (product or service) before?

When the lead-in question doesn't produce the desired response, it's appropriate to ask a second lead-in question. There are even times when several lead-in questions might be asked. What you are trying to do is get the customer interested. Here's an exchange with several lead-ins in a row:

CSR: How did you hear about us?

CUSTOMER: I'm not sure. (Not much of a response.)

CSR: Have you used our XYZ Flyer before?

CUSTOMER: No. (Oops, things aren't going very well.)

CSR: How do you plan to use our XYZ Flyer?

CUSTOMER:	Our marketing group is interested. They think it might help their productivity. (Bingo!)
CSR:	Several of our customers are using the XYZ Flyer in a sales or a marketing environment. In fact, we have conducted some research, and the results show some interesting productivity increases. I can briefly summarize the research for you. Do you have a moment?
CUSTOMER:	Yes, I'm very interested in that.
CSR:	Good. Well, first of all, . . .

In this situation, the CSR asked three lead-in questions before the customer expressed an interest in further conversation. Sometimes it takes that many—you have to remain patient and keep the tone conversational as you pursue the desired information. Of course, it's also important to listen to the customer. If you get little interest or no response, it's time to end the call.

THE COMPANION STATEMENT/QUESTION

Let's return to our chasing-the-rabbit example in order to study the concept of companion statements. After the CSR asked, "How do you plan to use our XYZ Flyer?", the customer responded with information about her marketing department's interest is improving productivity. The next response by the CSR is called a companion statement. This statement about other customers who are using the XYZ Flyer in a sales or marketing environment also mentions the productivity research the CSR's organization has conducted. She asks if the customer is interested, and he is. The lead-in question worked, and the companion statement that followed also worked. The CSR has successfully engaged the customer in conversation about the product.

In our example, the customer mentioned *productivity*—that was the key word that triggered the CSR's companion statement. CSRs must have companion statements/questions prepared in advance and mentally scripted for feedback to the customer. Unless you're ready with a response, there is little point in asking the lead-in questions. Nearly every customer conversation presents opportunities for information gathering. The lead-in question finds the opportunity, and the companion statement or question explores and develops it.

HOW TO DEVELOP COMPANION STATEMENTS

Once a few lead-in questions have been developed and firmly recorded in your mind, it's time to create the companion statements for those lead-ins. Envisioning the responses to your lead-in questions isn't a difficult task, because in most situations the customer's responses will be easy to anticipate. For example, it's likely you will know how your product or service is going to be used. Here's an example of more lead-in and companion statements in the XYZ Flyer conversation:

CSR: If you purchase our XYZ Flyer, how do you plan to use it?

CUSTOMER: We thought it might work well for us on the factory floor.

Aha! The CSR has heard this response a zillion times before and has a standard, well-prepared, mentally scripted response ready to use. It will create interest from the customer and promote added conversation.

CSR: Many of our customers are using the XYZ Flyer in factory situations, and it's working well for them. They tell us that savings because of the inventory control features of the XYZ are close to 30%.

CUSTOMER: 30%! That's excellent! Is there documentation for those figures?

Again, the CSR anticipated that the customer would be interested in the documentation.

CSR:	Yes, BigLow Inc. and Rapid Tech were used as the research sites, and they have given us permission to share the findings. Shall I send you a copy?
CUSTOMER:	By all means. I didn't know Rapid Tech was one of your customers.
CSR:	As you'll see in the research, Rapid Tech is using two XYZs.
CUSTOMER:	Two? We were thinking just one.
CSR:	There are some definite benefits for using multiple XYZs. For example, . . .

And so it goes. The CSR used standard lead-in questions, and when she heard a "typical" response, the companion statement was ready. She used it, it worked, and now the customer is curious about two products instead of just one.

"HEY, WHAT'S GOING ON? THIS IS SALES STUFF!"

Earlier, we discussed the CSR fact-finding process as a high-end service effort rather than a sales activity. It's worth mentioning this difference again, now that we've studied various questioning techniques. Too often the skills of fact-finding, developing customer information, and exploring the opportunity to enhance an order are thought of as sales methods rather than service endeavors. Actually, fact-finding (or *probing,* as it's often called) fits into both the sales and service arenas.

The fact-finding process suggested here is to allow you, the CSR, to ask questions in an organized manner, to produce added customer information that may result in an upgraded order or future business. You are not usually responsible for sales; nevertheless, when it's appropriate, you should try to develop customer information and to explore the possibility for upgrading orders. Depending on your organization's structure, you may hand the customer information off to sales for follow-up, or you may be required to act upon the information yourself. But one way or another, remember that fact finding is an important and marketable skill for a CSR to learn and to put into practice. It increases your value as a CSR.

Exercise: Asking Questions and Fact-Finding

To get started developing your fact-finding ability, complete the following exercise.

The situation: A new customer calls and inquires about your products and your organization. She wants to know prices and availability. As the CSR, you answer her questions. You also want to learn more about this new customer and explore the possibility for added or future business.

1. *What lead-in questions would you like to ask? Make a list of at least six questions you would like to have answered.*

To formulate your questions, pick one of your actual customers and think about the type of customer information you would like to have from them. Assume they will answer any reasonable question if it is phrased properly and fits within the conversation.

Your lead-in questions:

1. _____

2. _____

3. _____

4. _____

5. _____

6. _____

2. *Now that you have a few lead-in questions, make a list of your companion statements or questions.*

Keep the customer's expected response in mind as you develop each companion statement. Also, think about what you want the customer to hear from you. For example, say the customer needs to hear about the specific benefits of a particular product or service. You therefore need to incorporate your benefits into the companion statements. Here are three examples:

- "As you may know, we were awarded the Number One industry service award for last year. You will find our service second to none." (Quality service is the benefit.)

- "The 712 and 819 models are faster than our competitor's, and the pricing is very competitive. How important is speed of operation to your organization?" (Speed of operation and pricing are the benefits.)

- "When you open an account with us, we provide—in addition to a monthly statement—a year-end summary. No one else offers as much detail in their year-end statements as we do. Would you like to see a sample year-end summary?" (Year-end summary is the benefit.)

NOTE: As you make your list of companion statements and questions, be sure to tie them to your lead-in questions. Think of the expected customer response to your lead-in question, and create a companion statement to coincide.

Your companion statements/questions:

1. _____

2. _____

3. _____

4. _____

5. _____

6. _____

Hang on to this list of lead-in questions and companion statements/ questions. Put them into practice; as you do, new questions and statements will develop. Before long you will have a comprehensive list of questions and statements that will enable you to consistently learn more about your customers. In addition, if part of your job is taking customer orders, you will see the average order value increase.

Always keep in mind that the more you know about your customer, and the more the customer knows about your products and organization, the greater the probability of an increased order. Your level of customer knowledge and customer service will improve together—it's a win-win situation.

SKILL 7: PRODUCT KNOWLEDGE

Some CSRs work in a commodity environment, where product knowledge is not critical. The customer in this market readily understands the products he or she is purchasing. As a result, there is little the CSR can add to the transaction. In other settings, CSRs may seldom need to talk about the benefits of their products, how they work, or their application. The CSR/customer dialogue is concerned with orders, time frames, backlogs, expedites, and nearly everything else *but* explaining the product.

For the vast majority of CSRs, however, a high level of product knowledge is one of the "must haves" of customer service. It's nearly impossible to function effectively without it. Try doing fact-finding during the customer conversation without product knowledge; it simply won't go very far. Try discussing the benefits of your product with a customer when your product knowledge is mediocre. It's difficult, if not impossible, to satisfy your customer if product knowledge is lacking.

Let's define what product knowledge means to the CSR.

Product Knowledge: Understanding *all* aspects of the product or service. This includes how the product works, it's application, the benefits, its limitations, the methods of delivery and implementation, and the pricing options. In short, product knowledge to a CSR means the ability to answer nearly any customer question about the product.

QUALITY SERVICE REQUIRES PRODUCT KNOWLEDGE

The greater your product knowledge, the easier it is to provide quality service. Let's say you have invented a bicycle. You designed the bicycle, built it, prepared a marketing plan, and established service policies. After six months of hard work, you meet with a group of customers to discuss the bicycle. Can you imagine a customer question you couldn't answer during this meeting? Armed with this level of knowledge, providing quality service should be fairly easy. This is exactly the type of knowledge most CSRs need.

WAYS TO DEVELOP EXCELLENT PRODUCT KNOWLEDGE

Since CSRs don't create the products and services of the organization, they must find other ways to acquire their product knowledge. Here are a few ideas to help you along in this task.

Training: Ideally, your organization will offer product training. Your responsibility is to commit to the training and take full advantage of it. Other training may be offered by manufacturers of the products you support. Supervisors, managers, and coworkers are other sources of training. In many situations they can provide valuable one-on-one training.

Brochures and Other Literature: Collateral material, usually designed for customers, can be a good source. This material normally features statements of product benefits that you can use when talking to a customer. The product application is usually described here, as well. *Note:* Your customers will formulate many of their questions from reading this material, so be prepared for the customer's questions by being familiar with the literature.

Other Departments or Work Units: Typically there are product experts within the organization. These people may work in production, engineering, sales, customer service, or another work group. Identify these sources and find one or two who are willing to help. It's the "let me pick your brain" approach.

Industry Sources: Often the CSR provides service to customers who are from the same industry. In this case, it's fairly easy to gather industry publications and learn about the industry.

Reading: There is no substitute for reading about your products and services. Find out about the corporate library, file drawers of information, technical reference material, annual reports, and other sources. Then use them.

CAREER TIP:

Remember, the responsibility for excellent product knowledge rests with you. A consistent effort to stay informed regarding your products and services is key to your ability to provide quality service and it enhances your value as a CSR.

THE PRODUCT KNOWLEDGE TEST

To test your knowledge of the products/services you support, rate yourself on a scale of 1 to 5.

	Not At All	Somewhat			Very Well
Do I understand how the product works?	1	2	3	4	5
Can I describe the product or service to customers?	1	2	3	4	5
Can I answer nearly every customer question about the product?	1	2	3	4	5
Do I understand the key applications of the product?	1	2	3	4	5
Can I describe the benefits of the product?	1	2	3	4	5
Do I understand the service policies associated with the products?	1	2	3	4	5
Do I thoroughly understand the product pricing and billing options?	1	2	3	4	5
(If appropriate) Can I compare my product to those of my competitors?	1	2	3	4	5

THE BENEFITS OF CSR PRODUCT KNOWLEDGE

The benefits of product knowledge are numerous. When you are armed with extensive product knowledge, good things happen. You'll be able to

- Explain products to the customer
- Understand the customer's product application
- Clearly state the benefits of the product for the customer
- Compare your product with the competition's
- Offer advice and counsel to the customer
- Create larger orders
- Do more effective fact finding
- Be of greater service to the customer

SKILL 8: WORKING TOWARD A STRONGER RELATIONSHIP

The CSR's goal to satisfy the customer is accomplished in part by developing a strong relationship with that customer. What is a "strong" relationship?

> **Strong Customer Relationship:**   A relationship between the CSR and the customer, based on trust, mutual respect, rapport, and the shared goal of customer satisfaction.

RELATIONSHIPS DEVELOP

Typically, we think of building a strong customer relationship as being accomplished over a period of time. The CSR continually provides service, the customer comes to rely on that service, and a relationship develops. A strong relationship can also develop quickly, however, in just one or two customer conversations.

- The customer calls an 800 number. You answer, and over the course of the next few minutes demonstrate good product knowledge and offer some excellent advice.

- Maybe the customer calls to inquire about a particular product or service. Instead of just responding to the questions, you conduct some fact-finding and discover the customer doesn't need the high-priced model but can use the lower-priced model effectively. The customer is very satisfied, and saves money because you learned about her needs, knew the product application, and suggested a thriftier alternative.

- Suppose your fact finding reveals the customer does need the higher-priced model. The customer is still satisfied because you guided him toward ordering the right product.

In our examples, how do you think the customer views the association with the CSR? At a very minimum, the customer sees the relationship as a positive one. With only one conversation, the customer is satisfied. He knows you can be trusted, are knowledgeable, care about his business, will take the time to learn about his needs, and are someone he can depend on. When you take time—even a few minutes—to ask questions about the customer's business and product application, you acquire a better understanding of your customer. Armed with that knowledge, you are building a strong relationship.

BE CONSISTENT

Proving to your customers that they can depend on you is essential to developing customer-service relationships. Another cornerstone of a strong customer/CSR association is the *consistency* of your service level. The last thing a customer wants is a yo-yo type of relationship, where your service varies from excellent and reliable on one occasion, to poor and inaccurate the next. To build a strong customer relationship, you must demonstrate that your service will be delivered consistently.

MAKING THE CUSTOMER YOUR CLIENT

We have seen that, in order to build a strong relationship, the CSR must be accurate, knowledgeable, trustworthy, and provide consistent service. When this happens, the customer gets what he or she wants and as a result finds the relationship satisfying. Because you have formed a valuable relationship, the customer becomes your *client.* Sometimes we think of a client as someone served by an attorney, accountant, or other business professional. Your customers can become clients, too—if you provide added value to the relationship. When you provide advice and counsel along with problem-solving support and consistency, you bring substantial value to the association with the customer, and the relationship changes. You and your customer begin to function as partners. You work together to solve problems and make decisions. The customer no longer acts independently in his or her decision making, but relies on you for additional valuable input and advice.

The two examples that follow illustrate a customer relationship as compared to a client relationship. The contrast between the two is very clear.

TRACY MANAGES THE INQUIRY FOR HER CUSTOMER

Tracy receives a call from Karen Good, a longtime customer. Tracy and Karen have a good working relationship; Their conversation goes like this:

TRACY: How may I help you?

KAREN: I hear your prices have changed. Is that true?

TRACY: Yes, but they don't go into effect until the first of the month.

KAREN: How much did you lower them?

TRACY: (laughing) Now Karen, you know better than that.

KAREN: (also amused) That's what I figured. I guess I'd better get a few orders in. We like to save where we can.

TRACY: I'm ready. What do you need?

Tracy takes the order, thanks Karen for her business, and ends the conversation. Many CSRs have customer relationships very similar to this one—relationships in which much of the formality of doing business has been replaced by a friendly and cordial association. When CSRs establish this type of relationship with a large number of their customers, they can be pleased with their effort and will see good results.

TRACY IS A RESOURCE FOR HER CLIENT

Although Tracy and Karen are friendly and on good terms, their relationship is not a client/CSR relationship. Here's an illustration of the difference:

TRACY: Hi. I thought I would call and let you know how our new price changes may affect you.

KAREN: I heard the news. How much are you lowering them?

TRACY: (laughing) Now, you know better than that.

KAREN: That's what I figured.

TRACY: I was thinking—this price change is an opportunity for you to save some money by ordering before the changes go into effect.

KAREN: I thought about that, but I only have a few orders I can place now.

TRACY: What about the new service for your manufacturing group?

KAREN: I haven't heard from them. They probably haven't decided.

TRACY: Well, I figured out their savings. If they order before the new prices go into effect they can save nearly $2,000.

KAREN: I didn't think it would be that much. I'm not sure they're ready, anyway.

TRACY: What we can do is place the order, which will secure the savings, and I can hold delivery for up to 60 days.

KAREN: Their objection will be the future commitment. If they buy your service, they are locked in and have to purchase all the upgrades from you. I don't think they are ready to decide.

TRACY: If you don't mind my asking, what other service have they considered?

KAREN: Some of the engineers like the Champion System. Now that you have raised your prices, they will be even more interested.

TRACY: Our system has proven to be much more reliable than Champion's.

KAREN: I agree. That study you showed me was impressive.

TRACY: Champion also raised their prices.

KAREN: I didn't know that. By how much, do you know?

TRACY: I hear it's 20%, but I don't feel comfortable quoting their prices. Why don't we check with them?

KAREN: That's a good idea. If Champion raised their prices by 20%, I think manufacturing might be more interested in your service. Let me get a new quote from Champion, and I'll get back to you.

Obviously, her client sees Tracy as a valuable resource. They are on the same side, and they both believe manufacturing should install Tracy's system. Their conversation is between two people working together toward the same end.

CONVERTING YOUR CUSTOMERS TO CLIENTS

The customer-to-client conversion process takes place when you do the following:

- Become a consistent problem solver for the customer.
- Create trust by being accurate and knowledgeable.
- Take ownership of the customer's problems and concerns.
- Understand the customer's needs and issues.
- Never surprise the customer.
- Level with the customer.
- Demonstrate competence.
- Worry with the customer.
- Be innovative.
- Maintain confidentiality.
- Be motivated.
- Be flexible.
- Treat the customer/client like a person.

When all of this occurs, you become a valuable resource to your client. For example, Karen knows that if her company purchases Tracy's system they also get the high-level service Tracy consistently provides. When competing prices and other factors are similar, the CSR's level of service can be the deciding factor.

How many clients, as opposed to customers, do you have? How many of your customers can you develop into clients? Think about the relationships between you and each of your customers. Is it an adversary relationship? Hopefully not! Is it strictly a customer talking with a CSR? How much help, beyond the normal standard expected, do you provide for your customers? Look again at the customer-to-client conversion factor, and set up goals for converting all your customers into clients. Your reward—and your clients' reward—will be a new level of customer satisfaction.

Remember—a customer doesn't become a client just because you're on friendly terms. The client must readily see that you bring additional value to the relationship.

SKILL 9: DEVELOPING AND IMPLEMENTING AN ACTION PLAN

Customers have ongoing problems and issues that require resolution. Usually, *action plans* are the way CSRs resolve these concerns for their customers.

There are two types of action plans. First, there's the internal action plan. It details all the actions a CSR is going to take within the supporting organization to resolve a customer issue. The customer is not involved, other than to hear the results.

It might be that meetings are needed to coordinate a solution. Sometimes new procedures have to be developed, or perhaps the CSR's management must review the situation and make a decision. Whatever the internal circumstances, the customer is typically protected from them.

As a general rule, you need not share internal information with the customer unless it's of a very positive nature. Certainly confidential information should never be shared. Internal problems, especially, are best kept in house.

The second type of action plan comes into play when the CSR decides to resolve a customer problem or issue by developing an action plan in conjunction with the client. Here's an example of how that would work.

Shannon's Plan

Shannon's customer, Bill Davis, expressed considerable dissatisfaction with response times to his inquiries of Shannon's organization. Mr. Davis cited numerous incidents in which customer service or the salesperson had promised a quick response but failed to deliver. Shannon and Mr. Davis discussed the situation thoroughly so she could better understand the problem. She then asked him what he thought a reasonable response time would be. He said, "Other than urgent situations, I expect same-day responses on most questions, and next-day on more complex inquiries."

Shannon told her client that his demands were certainly reasonable, and promised to look into the situation. "Let me see what kind of a solution I can offer you. If I call you back Friday morning, with some feedback, will that be soon enough?" Davis agreed.

Shannon has made a commitment to find a solution for her organization's slow response times. Where should she begin? What sort of action plan should Shannon develop? Before answering these questions, let's look at a few ideas on how to create and structure an action plan.

ANATOMY OF AN ACTION PLAN

There are three important components of any action plan:

- It must show ownership.
- It must be workable.
- It must satisfy the customer.

The CSR takes ownership of the plan by accepting the responsibility to develop and implement it. Obviously, the plan must be workable—one that can actually be implemented. There is little point in creating a plan that is too long-range or too ambitious to succeed. Action plans usually center around some sort of customer dissatisfaction, and it's foolish to risk further customer dissatisfaction by establishing a plan that may not work. Customer satisfaction is the goal of any action plan.

THE CUSTOMER'S ROLE IN THE ACTION PLAN

The standard role of the customer is to approve the action plan. The CSR presents the action plan, with its design to resolve the customer's problem or issue. During this process, you ask the customer for input and then make needed changes in order to get the customer's approval. Next, the customer is usually assigned the role of providing feedback. Other customer roles might be identifying expected outcomes, adding forecasts, or issuing future orders.

Some action plans may include a request for the customer to behave or operate differently. For example, suppose a customer complains about delivery intervals. The solution might be for the customer to place the orders sooner. In this situation, tactfully explain to the customer *how* the delays can be reduced. Show how you can help the customer develop accurate forecasts, so that orders can be issued sooner. The only limitation to your client's role in the action plan is your imagination.

Whether the action plan is basic or complex, a crucial role for the customer is indicating the level of satisfaction at the outcome. It's common, and tempting, for CSRs and others to pronounce the customer satisfied without first getting verification from the customer. In *all* situations, however, the customer is the one who decides when this has happened. It may be a simple "Thanks for taking care of this" or "I appreciate your quick response." When the level of a customer's satisfaction is not clear, it's time to ask. "Are you satisfied with this response?" or "Does that solve all aspects of the problem for you?" Asking customers about their level of satisfaction is part of quality service.

CONSTRUCTING THE ACTION PLAN

Let's return to Shannon and her action plan for her customer. To structure it, she should consider the following eight steps, and use any or all of them as needed for her action plan:

1. WHO is responsible?

2. WHAT is going to happen?

3. WHEN will it happen?

4. WHERE will it happen?

5. HOW will it happen?

6. WHAT are the benefits to the customer?

7. WHY will it happen?

8. COMMUNICATE the plan to the customer.

WHO is responsible? Although Shannon will bear the primary responsibility for developing and implementing the action plan, she needs to get her Sales group involved. Her first step is to meet with the Sales manager to discuss the situation. The Sales manager agrees to be more responsive to the customer by assigning a specific salesperson to the account. The Sales manager also agrees that any service situations should be handed over to Shannon for her follow-up. Shannon feels these actions will give her more control.

WHAT is going to happen?   Shannon now has a commitment from the Sales manager. Her next action is to meet with the Engineering coordinator. She explains, during this meeting, that the customer is not satisfied with inquiry response times. Also, Shannon informs the coordinator that she is constantly waiting for Engineering to provide feedback regarding Bill Davis' inquiries. She tells the coordinator, "I can't respond to the customer quickly enough because I'm always waiting for you to call me." Following much discussion and persuasion, Shannon gets the coordinator to agree to improve the response times on Davis' inquiries and issues.

WHEN will it happen? The Engineering coordinator and the Sales manager have agreed to immediately improve their respective response times.

WHERE will it happen?   (not applicable in this situation)

HOW will it happen?   Shannon decides she will monitor every inquiry from the customer and its response time. The assigned salesperson agrees to do the same. Shannon also includes as part of the plan that she will periodically ask Davis about his level of satisfaction with the response times. In addition to checking with the customer and the salesperson, she will keep the Engineering coordinator informed of the level of customer satisfaction.

WHAT are the benefits to the customer?   The customer gets what he wants: improved response times, allowing him to be more effective in his job. With the faster response time, he will be able to respond more quickly to the people to whom he passes the information.

WHY will it happen?   The customer is dissatisfied. Dissatisfied customers have a habit of taking their business elsewhere. A successful action plan may prevent this from happening.

COMMUNICATE the plan to the customer.   This step is critical to the success of the action plan. When it's appropriate, the customer must be asked to approve the action plan and to participate in it. Let's see how Shannon communicates her plan to Bill Davis.

SHANNON: I wanted to let you know that I have taken steps to meet your time frames.

BILL DAVIS: Good. What did you come up with?

SHANNON: First let's talk about the Sales group and their response times. We have decided to assign a sales rep to your account. So, when you have an inquiry, you can call one person who will help you. This will dramatically speed up your response times.

BILL DAVIS: That's great. I didn't think our account was large enough for an assigned salesperson.

SHANNON: You're an important account for us and we want to see you satisfied. The new salesperson's name is Kimberly Morgan. She will call you on Monday to make an appointment for the two of you to meet.

BILL DAVIS: Good. I'll look forward to her call.

SHANNON: Regarding my own response times, I've made a few changes. I can meet your request for same-day response times on most issues, and next-day response time for the more complex questions. I'm going to make that my goal.

BILL DAVIS: Good. I know there will be times when you can't get back to me on the same day. When that happens, let me know in advance.

SHANNON: I'll do that. I do need your help in making all this work.

BILL DAVIS: Sure. What can I do?

SHANNON: I'm going to track my response times so that I'll know where we stand at all times. I'd like you to do the same. Periodically, at least once a month, we can discuss the situation and determine your level of satisfaction.

BILL DAVIS: That's a good idea. That should work well for us.

SHANNON: I'm positive this plan will work for us. Are you comfortable with everything we've talked about?

BILL DAVIS: Yes. I think it's a solid plan.

In a short telephone call, Shannon presented her action plan. It is workable and, when implemented, should satisfy the customer.

ACTION PLAN EMPOWERMENT

Shannon's action plan involved the Sales manager and the Engineering coordinator. She knew she couldn't satisfy the customer without them. Shannon could have taken the position that she wasn't responsible for the Sales manager's effort. She might also have said, "I can't change the slow response times from Engineering." Instead she convinced the Engineering coordinator of the need for improved response times. This team approach will go a long way toward resolving her customer's problem.

Most CSRs depend on internal sources—Operations, Sales, Marketing, Shipping, Accounting, other CSRs, and of course company management—for the information they pass on to their customers. To be successful, the CSR needs input and cooperation from these other work units. When the organization is customer focused, it's a simple matter for the CSR to get help and support just by saying "The customer isn't satisfied." When this happens the discussion can be used to determine how to correct the situation. However, this is not always the case. There are times and situations when the CSR must step forward in an empowered manner and demand support. Using good judgment, as discussed earlier, the CSR must alert the organization to the fact that a customer is not satisfied.

Groups and departments within a business that never see or hear a real customer need to be reminded of the customer's importance to the organization. The CSR, among others, is automatically empowered to do that. Developing and implementing customer action plans is an important way to involve these employees and work units. In our example, Shannon involved Engineering in her action plan. Though the Engineering coordinator never speaks directly with customers, she plays a vital support role in providing customer service. She provides dates, schedules, and other information to the CSR, who in turn delivers these to the customer. Perhaps in your organization, someone like the coordinator is not as customer focused as you and the salesperson are. In some situations, non-customer service personnel may be completely focused internally and may even regard you, the CSR, as a nuisance. You may be struggling with a view that says, "These are the dates and schedules. The customer will have to accept them."

When confronted with such an attitude, it's your job to remind people that customer satisfaction is what keeps the organization running and pays everyone's salary. One way to do this is to get people like the Engineering coordinator involved in the action plan. Assign them a role. Get their agreement to act in a customer-focused manner. When appropriate, involve them in customer meetings. Employees and managers who are not in contact with the customer usually need a consistent reminder of their importance to the customer. The CSR must continually carry this message.

SKILL 10: SMALLER ACTION PLANS

Shannon's action plan was somewhat complex. In everyday situations, smaller action plans are needed as well. To provide assurance for the customer, an action plan need not be complicated. Sometimes these action plans simply explain to the customer the steps to be taken to resolve customer issues or problems.

SIMPLE APPROACH

Simple, basic action plans tell the customer that you understand the problem and are going to do something about it. Your responsibility, as always, is to understand the customer's needs and formulate an appropriate response.

For example, when you have a strong relationship with the customer, you might be able to just say "I'll take care of it." In this circumstance, the customer knows from past experience to depend on your word. When you know that a more detailed response is required, you might add, "First, I'll call Accounting and find out why they billed it this way. Next, I'll talk with them about sending a new invoice. I'll get back to you within the hour. Will that be all right?" When you know the customer is highly assertive and not too interested in the details, an appropriate action plan might be "I'll look into it and call you this afternoon."

Sometimes an apology may be in order as part of the action plan: "I'm sorry this happened. Here's what I can do for you." This doesn't admit a mistake was made, but apologizes in a general way. Often it's best to apologize and accept responsibility for creating the problem, but there are other times when this is not appropriate. You can nearly always say things like, "I'm sorry about this situation" or "I'm sorry this caused such a problem for you." There are countless ways to show empathy; and one way is to offer a general apology for the situation.

Quite often, customers need information to pass on to others within their organizations—even in simple situations. That means even the basic action plan must be completely accurate. Provide known information, keeping speculation of what may occur to a minimum. An inaccurate action plan may cause your client embarrassment. Smaller action plans may be basic, but they are still important. Customers want to work with CSRs who take responsibility for solving problems and addressing issues. Implementing even the most basic action plan means taking responsibility.

SKILL 11: SELF-APPRAISAL

It can generally be said of successful CSRs that they understand their strengths and weaknesses and strive for continued improvement. If you have read this book to this point, you are probably interested in self-improvement. The great difficulty for most CSRs is to accurately conduct an ongoing self-appraisal to determine strengths and areas of concern. Self-appraisals require honesty of the highest order and as much objectivity as possible. Self-improvement then becomes an ongoing process.

Three Steps to Self-Improvement

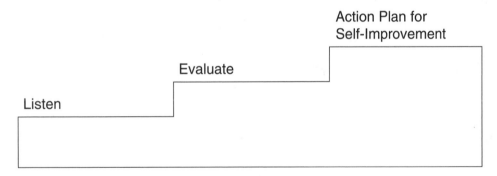

STEP 1: LISTEN

As shown in the chart above, the first step toward self-appraisal involves listening critically to our own customer conversations. The next step is to evaluate what we hear. The final step is to develop and implement an action plan for self-improvement. Of course, objectivity is critical while you're completing the three steps. This is not an easy task by any means. Let's look at obstacles that typically stand in the CSR's path to self-improvement.

ROADBLOCKS TO SELF-IMPROVEMENT

One of the key obstacles is *ego*. Individual *egos* get right in the middle of our best intentions. We intend to conduct a searching self-appraisal so that we can improve our performance. As we proceed, if we're objective, we may become aware of our interfering egos. Frequently, egos are so strong that we're not even aware of the absence of objectivity. Egos cloud performance evaluation, but only if we let them.

In addition to egos, distractions—both personal and professional—get in the way of our objectivity. Often, these distractions are so great we can't hear our own conversation with the customer. At other times, we are busy mentally, anticipating what the customer's next question or statement will be. As a result, we fail to hear ourselves, and objectivity becomes impossible. Let's look at a typical example.

Allen Decides He's a Strong Performer

Allen has considerable customer service experience and sees himself as a strong performer. In the past, he has not welcomed criticism, no matter how constructive. He is very positive about his CSR experience and honestly thinks he's a top performer.

At the suggestion of his boss, Allen conducts a self-appraisal. He begins by listening closely to each one of his many customer calls and making notes as he proceeds. Allen reviews his notes on 50 calls and concludes he is handling the calls expertly. He is unable to identify any areas for self-improvement.

Allen meets with his boss, Susan, and reports his findings. Susan listens carefully, and then asks, "How do you rank yourself with the other CSRs?" Allen replies that he feels he's in the top 10%. When asked why he ranks himself so high, Allen cites his experience.

Susan is rather direct with Allen and tells him that she and the other managers disagree. "You work hard and do your share, but your order accuracy is poor. I don't think you're listening to your customers as well as you could." Susan cites several recent examples of incorrect orders and goes on to explain that this is not acceptable for top CSRs. Allen responds by stating that many of his customers are non-native speakers and are hard for him to understand. "They often change their minds after they place an order", he says. Susan explains that all the CSRs work with non-native speaking customers and manage to complete accurate orders.

She asks Allen, "Are you using the non-native speaker skills and techniques from our company training?" Allen says he is. Susan asks him to re-examine his 50 calls and determine how many customers were non-native speakers. Next, she asks him to think about how well he listened to these customers, and whether he used the non-native speaker skills he had learned in training. Allen replies that he does listen closely and always uses the new skills. Susan asks him to think about it some more and that they will meet again to discuss the issue.

Allen is stuck. He sees his performance much differently than Susan and the other managers do. He also seems to lack objectivity when his failure to listen closely to customers is pointed out. What is Allen's roadblock to an honest self-appraisal? It may be ego, which doesn't allow him to see his weakness. Maybe he has an individual bias toward non-native speaking customers. Perhaps it's something else. But if Allen is serious about self-improvement, he'll have to remove his ego from the situation. He must recognize where improvement is needed and then determine what is holding him back. When trying to listen to themselves, many CSRs will struggle with objectivity just as Allen did.

Frequently, the roadblock is just the inability to hear the customer conversation. When you're in the midst of a conversation with a customer and doing fact-finding or taking an order, it's indeed difficult to evaluate every action and statement. Taping the customer conversation and then replaying it can help, if that's possible in your operation. If you want an accurate self-appraisal, you'll have to simply tune in and hear yourself.

STEP 2: EVALUATE

In terms of self-evaluation, attitude is often a major roadblock for CSRs seeking self-improvement. You'll need courage to recognize when attitude is the roadblock to self-improvement. However, it can be done. Attitude, to a large extent, is a choice we make. We can choose to be customer focused and to work on self-improvement.

Your attitude will definitely play a role. If your attitude is open and receptive to change, then self-improvement will occur. If your attitude is negative and close-minded, there is little chance for success.

A self-appraisal guideline can be used during the customer conversation or immediately following. This guideline will differ by organization. You'll find a suggested guideline below.

CSR Self-Appraisal

Circle One

1. Did I welcome the customer to our organization?   **YES**   **NO**

    How did I do this? What did I say? _____

2. Did I understand the customer's problem, issue,   **YES**   **NO**
    or request?

3. Did I offer an appropriate response?   **YES**   **NO**

    What did I say? _____

Circle One

4. Was the customer satisfied with my response?   YES   NO

How did the customer indicate satisfaction? _____

5. *When taking an order:*

Did I get all the order information correct?   YES   NO

Did the customer have to repeat any of the information?   YES   NO

(If appropriate) Did I discuss or suggest other products?   YES   NO

6. *Communication Skills:*

Did I listen to the customer?   YES   NO

Was I courteous at all times?   YES   NO

Did I speak the customer's language and not mine (that is, did I avoid acronyms and organizational terminology?)   YES   NO

Did I build rapport with the customer?   YES   NO

Did I thank the customer for calling (or for the customer's business or order)?   YES   NO

7. *Action Plans:* (if required)

Did I present a workable action plan?   YES   NO

Did the customer approve the action plan?   YES   NO

8. Did I do fact finding for added business and more service to the customer?   YES   NO

What kind of questions did I ask? _____

Did I use lead-ins and companion statements/questions?   YES   NO

Circle One

9. Is the customer satisfied?   **YES   NO**

(If yes) How do I know the customer is satisfied? _____

(If no) Why isn't the customer satisfied? _____

Each self-appraisal format can differ based on the CSR's needs. In Allen's case, listening skills and the ability to work with non-native speakers would be emphasized. Allen, for example, might have the following questions on his appraisal:

Allen's Appraisal Questions

Circle One

	Circle One
Was the customer a non-native speaker?	**YES NO**
Did I listen closely?	**YES NO**
Did I use non-native speaker skills?	**YES NO**
When necessary, did I repeat myself exactly, and not paraphrase?	**YES NO**
Did I avoid slang and acronyms?	**YES NO**
Did I avoid expressions the customer might not know?	**YES NO**
Did I review the customer's order to make sure it was correct?	**YES NO**

STEP 3: ACTION PLAN FOR SELF-IMPROVEMENT

Once you define areas where improvement is needed, it's important to keep in mind that an action plan for improvement need not be complex. As mentioned earlier in the book, action plans can be very basic. For example, if listening is a problem area, the objectives might include counting the number of times the customer has to repeat information, or how often the CSR has to ask a question a second time.

Once objectives are identified, tracking them can help define a problem area, and also show the current level of CSR improvement.

As your CSR skills improve, the job gets easier and more rewarding. Listening, conducting a self-appraisal, and establishing an improvement plan is a sure way to upgrade your skills. A high CSR skill level also means less stress. When skills are strong, you take control and manage your job better. Being in control means fewer irate customers and a big reduction in those last-minute emergency situations.

V

MEASURING
CSR
PERFORMANCE

CSRs need a system for continually measuring and improving their performance. Ideally, this system will be a combination of self-appraisal and external input from a manager. By working together, the CSR and manager can accurately evaluate the CSR's performance. Then a Skill-Improvement Plan, when needed, can be created and implemented.

THE CSR EVALUATION SYSTEM

This section offers an evaluation system designed to assess performance on all skills of the CSR job. Space has been provided for CSRs and their organizations to add business skills or areas of knowledge specific to the organization.

The evaluation guide in this section can be used by the CSR alone as a self-evaluation tool without supervisor involvement; however, the guide will work best when both the CSR and manager participate. The evaluation system results should be used to identify the CSR strengths and weaknesses. Once the skill level identification takes place, a constructive improvement plan can be put into place, if needed. A Skill-Improvement Plan (SIP) is presented and discussed at the end of this section.

CSR EVALUATION SYSTEM

CSR: _____

SUPERVISOR: _____

DATE OF EVALUATION: _____

RATINGS:

> **5** = Mastery Of The Category
>
> **4** = Strong Performance
>
> **3** = Satisfactory Performance
>
> **2** = Less Than Satisfactory Performance
>
> **1** = Unsatisfactory Performance

CATEGORY 1: CUSTOMER COMMUNICATION SKILLS

Skill or Subject	Weight	CSR	Manager's	Final
Listening	____	____	____	____
Few, if any, errors are made due to poor listening. Customers do not have to repeat. The customer need is heard.				
Common Courtesy	____	____	____	____
The language used with the customer is consistently courteous.				
Ability to Probe (Fact Finding)	____	____	____	____
Can conduct fact finding with customer. Consistently develops needs and identifies opportunities for new customer orders.				

The Ratings (1–5) heading spans the Weight, CSR, Manager's, and Final columns.

Skill or Subject	Ratings (1–5)			
	Weight	*CSR*	*Manager's*	*Final*
Ability to Manage Customer Conversations	___	___	___	___
Shows consistency. Manages conversations well. Builds rapport. Is conversational.				
Management of Customers	___	___	___	___
CSR demonstrates skill in managing angry, highly assertive or other difficult customers. Knows how to calm these customers and identify and satisfy their needs.				
Other Skills:	___	___	___	___
_____				
_____				
_____				

Category Rating [＿＿＿＿＿]

CATEGORY 2: PROFESSIONALISM

Skill or Subject	Ratings (1–5)			
	Weight	*CSR*	*Manager's*	*Final*
Managing Workload	___	___	___	___
Effectively manages workload in a consistent manner. Meets deadlines. Plans daily activities. Avoids crises.				

Skill or Subject	Ratings (1–5)			
	Weight	CSR	Manager's	Final
Self-Managing	___	___	___	___
Manages job responsibilities with a minimum of management assistance or supervision.				
Empowerment	___	___	___	___
Consistently shows good judgement in resolving customer problems and executing responsibilities. Acts on behalf of the customer with a minimum of management assistance. Assumes responsibility for customer satisfaction.				
Time Management	___	___	___	___
Demonstrates good time management skills. Plans each day. Can manage a varied workload. Avoids time crises. Meets deadlines. Employs a time-management system that works.				
Self-Improvement	___	___	___	___
Continually works toward self-improvement. Has a SIP in place and shows progress.				
Other Skills:	___	___	___	___

_____

_____

_____

Category Rating [   ]

CATEGORY 3: CUSTOMER SATISFYING SKILLS

Skill or Subject	Ratings (1–5)			
	Weight	*CSR*	*Manager's*	*Final*
Customer Action Plans	____	____	____	____

Successfully develops and implements customer action plans. Creates workable plans. Involves customers when needed. Successfully includes other work units in implementation. Action plans produce customer satisfaction.

Proactivity	____	____	____	____

CSR is proactive in working with customers, responds in a timely manner to customer requests, takes initiative and acts on customer's behalf in advance of customer request to do so. Keeps customers informed. Advises customers in advance of changes.

Customer Knowledge	____	____	____	____

Demonstrates understanding of customer needs, modifies to meet specific customer personality needs. Understands how we (the organization) affect the customer's business, understands the application for our products.

Customer Relationships	____	____	____	____

Develops and maintains strong customer relationships. Has established a client-style relationship with most key accounts. Customers depend on and trust his/her advice and service.

Skill or Subject	Ratings (1–5)			
	Weight	CSR	Manager's	Final
Meets Customer Commitments	⎯⎯	⎯⎯	⎯⎯	⎯⎯
Customer commitments are kept, promised follow-ups are delivered, customer callbacks are made. Customer time frames are met.				
Other Skills:	⎯⎯	⎯⎯	⎯⎯	⎯⎯
⎯⎯⎯⎯⎯⎯⎯⎯⎯⎯⎯⎯⎯⎯⎯				
⎯⎯⎯⎯⎯⎯⎯⎯⎯⎯⎯⎯⎯⎯⎯				
⎯⎯⎯⎯⎯⎯⎯⎯⎯⎯⎯⎯⎯⎯⎯				

Category Rating ☐

CATEGORY 4: TEAMWORK SKILLS

Skill or Subject	Ratings (1–5)			
	Weight	CSR	Manager's	Final
Team Participation	⎯⎯	⎯⎯	⎯⎯	⎯⎯
CSR is an active member of the team, acts in the best interest of the team, participates in discussions, and adds value to team activities.				
Team Responsibilities	⎯⎯	⎯⎯	⎯⎯	⎯⎯
Accepts responsibility for team assignments. Meets deadlines and team commitments. Can be counted on to do his/her share or more.				

Skill or Subject	Ratings (1–5)			
	Weight	*CSR*	*Manager's*	*Final*
Team Decision Making	____	____	____	____
Participates in team decisions, is active in discussions, presents logical arguments and discussion. Stays focused during decision-making process. Listens to others. Supports the team decision.				
Teamwork	____	____	____	____
Promotes teamwork within the organization. Cooperates and works well with others. Is a positive force for teamwork				
Other Skills:	____	____	____	____
_____				
_____				
_____				

Category Rating [   ]

CATEGORY 5: ADMINISTRATIVE SKILLS

Skill or Subject	Ratings (1–5)			
	Weight	*CSR*	*Manager's*	*Final*
Orders	____	____	____	____
Understands order-entry system and procedures, is accurate, and makes few errors. Orders are completed and entered in acceptable time frames.				

Skill or Subject	Ratings (1–5)			
	Weight	CSR	Manager's	Final
Reports	___	___	___	___
Is thorough and concise in completing all reports. Meets deadlines.				
Customer Communications	___	___	___	___
Understands the appropriate use of fax, e-mail, other customer memos/letters. Messages are clear and well written. Manages voice-mail system well. Personally answers most customer calls. Changes "greetings" as needed. "Greetings" are accurate as to time of return, etc. Mailbox is effectively managed.				
Systems and Software	___	___	___	___
Understands computer system and is effective in using CSR-related software programs and procedures. Is generally self-sufficient and requires little outside help.				
Other Skills:	___	___	___	___
_____				
_____				
_____				

Category Rating [   ]

RATINGS

This evaluation system rates CSR skills in five categories. Following each skill, the CSR is asked to rate him/herself. Next to the CSR rating, the manager or supervisor places their rating. The rating should reflect how well the CSR's performance satisfies the skill. If the job performance is nearly identical to the description, then a high rating may be warranted. If job performance is very different from the description, then a lower rating applies. All ratings are on a 1–5 scale:

5 = Mastered

4 = Strong performer

3 = Satisfactory

2 = Less than satisfactory

1 = Unsatisfactory

WEIGHTING DESIRABLE OR IMPORTANT SKILLS

Each organization can weight particular skills as more or less valuable, depending on their needs. For example, in a category listing five skills, one or two of these may be perceived as more important than others. These weighted skills are to be noted on the form and they will influence the overall category ratings. Managers and CSRs may want to weight the evaluation items together. Within most organizations, the skills will be weighted the same for each CSR evaluation. Here's a weighting example.

EXAMPLE:

CSR: *Petra Smith*

Category: *Communications Skills*

	Weight	CSR	Manager	Final Rating
		Ratings		
Listening	2	3	3	6
Courtesy	1	5	4	4.5
Managing Objections	1	3	2	2.5
				13

- Category ratings Total is 13 ÷ 4 skills = 3.25

- Use 4 skills because Listening is weighted by 2; therefore, it counts as an extra skill.

Let's assume both the supervisor and CSR rate the CSR's Listening skills as a 3 (average). When computing the average rating for this category, the Listening weight of 2 is multiplied by the 3 rating, so 6 is written in the final average rating column. This 6 is to be used in figuring the average for the category. The overall category average is determined by dividing total ratings by number of skills.

A higher weight should be assigned when a skill is considered to be the most important within the category. For instance, in an organization that markets a complex product or service, CSR product knowledge might be weighted. In another organization, product knowledge might be less important because the customer automatically understands the product. Weighting in general should be kept to a minimum; it makes sense when requirements for skills or knowledge are well above average in a particular area. For the purposes of this example, a 1 is shown to make calculations clearer.

Note: Although weighting serves the purpose of emphasizing particular skills, it is not required in order to use this evaluation system. This system will work well without weighting.

DISCUSSING THE RATINGS

There are a variety of ways to conduct the CSR evaluation. One common method is for the CSR and manager to complete the rating, independently, and then meet to compare, discuss, and determine a final rating. Another method that can be effective is for the manager and CSR to jointly complete the ratings. Regardless of how the evaluation is done, the purpose is to identify the strengths and weaknesses of the CSR and develop an improvement plan if needed.

The CSR and the manager will not always agree on the individual skill ratings; this is to be expected. Work toward finding a common ground that is mutually acceptable. The key to the success of the evaluation system is strong communication between the CSR and manager. When the CSR desires a higher rating, there must be justification. Likewise, when the manager wants to give a low rating, there must be justification.

After individual ratings are discussed, an average rating for each category can be completed.

SKILL-IMPROVEMENT PLANS (SIP)

When the ratings fall below what the CSR and manager desire, a Skill-Improvement Plan (SIP) may be in order. A SIP is designed to identify activities for development of the CSR's skills. Activities are listed, reviewed with the CSR, and time frames for completion are established. When the SIP is completed, the CSR will have achieved the skills necessary to raise his rating in the evaluation system.

DEVELOPING AND IMPLEMENTING A SKILL-IMPROVEMENT PLAN

A SIP is basically a three-step process.

1. Based on the CSR evaluation, a particular skill is rated as needing improvement. Usually, any rating below a 3 (average) requires a SIP.

2. Next, a plan is created showing the activities to be completed by the CSR. The successful completion of these activities will lead to CSR improvement.

3. The final step is to monitor the level of improvement. This monitoring might be self-observation by the CSR or, ideally, a joint activity with management. The greater the interest expressed by management, the more successful the SIP will be.

THE KEYS TO SUCCESS

There are two keys to the success of any SIP. First, the CSR must be motivated to improve performance; second, the SIP must be realistic and workable. The SIP activities must have value and, when completed, lead to improvement. See the lay out of a SIP example on the following page.

SIP ATTACHMENT

Any SIP can also include an attachment that adds more detail or clarification to the improvement activities. When the skill area is well below average, a multitude of improvement activities and actual how-to details may be in order. The supervisor might create an attachment that describes the desired CSR behavior. Each item listed would include specific detail on what is to be done or learned, and the date by which progress must be shown. The clearer and more concise the activities, the greater the probability of success.

EXAMPLE:

SKILL-IMPROVEMENT PLAN (SIP)

CSR: Joe Smith

Date: _____

Skills Needing Improvement	Evaluation Rating	Improvement Activities and Objectives	Target Completion Date
Increase team participation	2	Participate in every team discussion, volunteer for special assignments. Improve rating to a 3.	June 12: show increased participation by this date
Time management	1	Must plan each day, reduce order delays and missed deadlines, provide more timely customer feedback. Improve rating to 3.	Improvement must be noted by July 20
Build stronger relationships with key accounts	3	Increase understanding of key account needs, improve customer feedback process, develop more complete and workable action plans, test for improvement by asking customer for input. Improve rating to a 4.	Begin immediately, show improvement by end of 2nd quarter. In four weeks, ask customers if improvement has been noticed.

VI

A MESSAGE
TO THE CSR

Earlier we discussed three key factors that produce satisfied customers. The third and most important factor is the frontline CSR. Even when the structure of service and management policies are less than ideal, the actions of the CSR can be the cornerstone of an overall successful relationship with customers.

You, the CSR, occupy this frontline position. You have a great deal to do with determining the customer's perception of the organization. Although salespeople and other customer-contact employees are important to this effort, often the daily and most significant customer-contact workload is carried by the CSR. The CSR may manage dozens of customer conversations in one day, take order after order, and resolve complex customer problems.

SKILLS, SKILLS, AND MORE SKILLS

Your future as a CSR is going to demand even more skill and knowledge. Customer needs will continue to change, and they will demand and expect more of their suppliers. The competition will get sharper. If you want a rewarding career in customer service, you must continue to prepare yourself for the future—because the skills and knowledge of today will not be enough for tomorrow.

High-end customer service jobs will require considerable product knowledge and problem-solving skills. Just answering the telephone and handling the inquiry won't get you one of these jobs, but education, skill, experience, and knowledge will. Every CSR who reads this book should have a SIP, as described in Section V. Set your goal as development of not just one or two skills, but to improve overall professionalism and knowledge. If, for example, you have a high-school diploma, take classes at a community college. If you have some college but no degree, get an Associate degree. Work toward a bachelor's degree or even start graduate work. Why? Because you are going to need it before your service career ends.

SUCCESS IS IN YOUR FUTURE

One requirement for success will be the CSR's ability to acquire and use new knowledge. Down the line, some employer is going to hire or promote you based on your proven ability to learn. Maybe it's a new system, an advanced product, or a unique problem-solving situation. Regardless of what has to be learned, your core knowledge will come into play—core knowledge gained from your experience, SIPs, education, and skill. The stronger your core knowledge, the greater your probability for success. If in five years you are still trying to get by on today's skills and education, it probably won't work for you. If in 10 or 15 years you are trying to do it, there's a guarantee it won't work.

THE IMPORTANCE OF THE CSR JOB

Service will continue to grow in importance in every industry, as will the CSR job. Customer service—once viewed as a stepping stone to other positions—is becoming a career. At the high-end there will be a thin line between the CSR, sales support, and inside sales positions. The trend in the high-end jobs now is for a blend of these positions and their responsibilities. The CSR meets with salespeople, makes customer calls, receives incoming customer calls, advises salespeople, counsels a customer, helps salespeople prepare presentations, solves complex customer problems, takes a large order, and then participates in a team meeting. During the team meeting, the CSR may wear all of these hats.

The CSR job carries responsibility, is seldom dull, pays well, and offers strong fringe benefits. It is not a dead end, answer the telephone only, position. It is a job with a future. It is a job you can have, if your skill, education, ability to learn, and knowledge are strong enough.

SOME THINGS WON'T CHANGE MUCH

Despite the changes we have discussed, there will be much that won't change. The high-volume and demanding workload will always be part of the CSR position. Stress will continue to be a factor. At times the CSR workload will mushroom because of high customer demand. But all of this is manageable. Knowledge and skill will carry you through the crises periods. With experience and continual skills improvement, the stress of the job will lessen and become even more manageable.

IT'S YOUR CHOICE!

So much of CSR success is guided by making the right choice at the right time. Sometimes it's as basic as saying, "I'll be positive during this busy period and not get involved in the office drama." Maybe it's more complex and you need to say, "I'm going to take some college classes as part of my SIP." Often you're made aware that customer satisfaction is slipping and it's time to do something about it.

With every situation there's a choice to be made. The thinking CSR considers the alternatives and makes the right choice. In most situations, the right choice is the one that benefits you, the organization, and the customer. In other circumstances, the right choice is the one that serves the best interest of the CSR's career and future. Sometimes, the right choice is just simply a display of a positive attitude. What a force that can be! As a CSR, especially when you're in the middle of a complex situation, think about the alternatives and options available. Think about what the average CSR might do—and then think about the road the outstanding CSR might follow. Narrow your choices down until only the positive ones are left.

APPLY THIS BOOK TO YOUR CAREER

The ideas and suggestions presented in this book will work for you and make you a stronger CSR. Using this knowledge is one of the choices you make. So get started! Put into practice what we've discussed here. Your career success is up to you. It's your choice.